Renaissance Men on Music

Books by David Whitwell

The Sousa Oral History Project
The Art of Musical Conducting
The Longy Club: 1900–1917
La Téléphonie and the Universal Musical Language
Extraordinary Women
A Concise History of the Wind Band
Essays on the Modern Wind Band
Essays on Performance Practice
A New History of Wind Music
The College and University Band
The Early Symphonies of Mozart
Music of the French Revolution
Stories from the Podium

On Composers
Wagner on Bands
Berlioz on Bands
Chopin: A Self-Portrait
Liszt: A Self-Portrait
Schumann: A Self-Portrait in His Own Words
Mendelssohn: A Self-Portrait in His Own Words

On Education
Philosophic Foundations of Education
Foundations of Music Education
Music Education of the Future

Aesthetics of Music
Aesthetics of Music in Ancient Civilizations
Aesthetics of Music in the Middle Ages
Aesthetics of Music in the Early Renaissance
Aesthetics of Music in Sixteenth-Century Italy, France and Spain
Aesthetics of Music in Sixteenth-Century Germany, the Low Countries and England
Aesthetics of Baroque Music in Italy, Spain, the German-Speaking Countries and the Low Countries
Aesthetics of Baroque Music in France
Aesthetics of Baroque Music in England

The History and Literature of the Wind Band and Wind Ensemble Series

Volume 1 The Wind Band and Wind Ensemble Before 1500
Volume 2 The Renaissance Wind Band and Wind Ensemble
Volume 3 The Baroque Wind Band and Wind Ensemble
Volume 4 The Wind Band and Wind Ensemble of the Classical Period (1750–1800)
Volume 5 The Nineteenth-Century Wind Band and Wind Ensemble
Volume 6 A Catalog of Multi-Part Repertoire for Wind Instruments or for Undesignated Instrumentation before 1600
Volume 7 Baroque Wind Band and Wind Ensemble Repertoire
Volume 8 Classical Period Wind Band and Wind Ensemble Repertoire
Volume 9 Nineteenth-Century Wind Band and Wind Ensemble Repertoire
Volume 10 A Supplementary Catalog of Wind Band and Wind Ensemble Repertoire
Volume 11 A Catalog of Wind Repertoire before the Twentieth Century for One to Five Players
Volume 12 A Second Supplementary Catalog of Early Wind Band and Wind Ensemble Repertoire
Volume 13 Name Index, Volumes 1–12, The History and Literature of the Wind Band and Wind Ensemble

Ancient Voices

Ancient Views on Music and Religion
Ancient Views on the Natural World
Ancient Views on What Is Music
Contemporary Descriptions of Early Musicians
Early Views of Music and Ethics
Early Thoughts on Performance Practice
Music Performance in Ancient Societies

Renaissance Voices

Essays on Renaissance Philosophies of Music
Renaissance Men on Music

www.whitwellbooks.com

David Whitwell

Renaissance Voices
Views on Music by Renaissance Writers

Renaissance Men on Music

Edited by Craig Dabelstein

WHITWELL PUBLISHING • AUSTIN, TEXAS, USA

Renaissance Voices: Views on music by Renaissance Writers
Renaissance Men on Music
Dr. David Whitwell

WHITWELL PUBLISHING
AUSTIN, TX 78701
WWW.WHITWELLPUBLISHING.COM

This volume is based on original essays published between 2000 and 2007.
© 2014 by David Whitwell
All rights reserved. First edition 2014

Composed in Bembo Book.
Published in the United States of America.
All images used in this book are in the public domain except where otherwise noted.

ISBN-13: 9781936512805

Cover design by Daniel Ferla.

Contents

	Acknowledgement	ix
1	Guillaume de Machaut on Music	1
2	Francesco Petrarch on Music	17
3	Giovanni Boccaccio on Music	35
4	Geoffrey Chaucer on Music	49
5	Leonardo da Vinci on Music	69
6	Baldassare Castiglione on Music	81
7	Michaelangelo on Art and Music	91
8	Girolamo Cardano on Music	99
9	Erasmus on Music	113
10	The Academies	131
	Bibliography	141
	About the Author	145
	About the Editor	147

Acknowledgments

I am indebted to my friend and colleague, Craig Dabelstein, for his help in preparing this book for publication.

David Whitwell
Austin, Texas

Guillaume de Machaut on Music

THE NAME OF GUILLAUME DE MACHAUT is written on the blackboard of every music history class following the chalk line which symbolizes the beginning of the Renaissance, in part, no doubt, because he was born on the chalk line, in 1300 (and died in 1377).[1] He was not only the most famous musician of fourteenth-century France, but also the most famous poet. Machaut's name was sufficiently well-known that even a century later, the author of a fifteenth-century hunting book in Portugal praised the noise of the hounds by stating that not even Guillaume de Machaut made such beautiful concordance of melody.

> Guilherme de Machado nom fez tam fermosa concordanca de melodia, nem que tam bem pareca como a fazem os ca—es quando bem correm.[2]

However, we are reasonably confident that Machaut would be quite astonished if he were brought back to life today to discover that his name was known primarily for a handful of compositions for the Church. That reputation is due not to the generosity, but to the narrowness of vision of nineteenth-century musicology.

We believe it much more appropriate to think of Machaut as the last troubadour. Much of his poetry praising nobles and their ladies is entirely in the tradition of the thirteenth century. In his love songs, however, the new themes of the Renaissance are present, in particular a greater emphasis on feeling. And it is clear that these songs in the tradition of the troubadour were very important to Machaut. He collected this music and carefully indexed it under the heading, 'This is the order which G. de Machaut wishes his book to have.'

> Vesci l'ordenance que .G. de Machau wet quil ait en son livre.[3]

We see another expression of this concern when, late in life, he sends a copy of a poem to his lover, Peronnelle. He pleas that she take good care of it, since he has no copy and would be distressed if it were lost, and were not 'in the book where I put all my things.'

---

[1] Machaut was probably educated at the cathedral school at Rheims and at the University of Paris. While still a young man be became associated with an important noble, John of Luxembourg, King of Bohemia. Machaut's reputation with other nobles can be seen in the fact that when Charles V visited Rheims a few years before the coronation, he advised the aldermen of the town to meet him 'chez maistre Guillyaume de Machault.' [Guillaume de Machaut, *Oeuvres*, ed. Ernest Hoepffner (Paris, 1908–21), I, xxv, xxxvff.]

[2] Quoted in Guillaume de Machaut, *Musikalische Werke*, ed. Friedrich Ludwig (Leipzig, 1926), II, 32.

[3] In this index, Mauchat lists separately by incipits each of his lais, motes, balades notes, rondeaulz and virelais in the music section and includes several hundred lyrics for ballades which have no music under the heading, 'Les balades ou il n'a point de chant.'

Before considering Machaut's views on music we should like first to provide some perspective on where he was positioned with respect to general philosophical questions of the fourteenth century. During the Middle Ages a frequent observation by philosophers was that we share our senses with lower animals, but not intellect. From this observation it followed that the senses must be a lower animal function, while intellect must be a special gift of God. When the first signs of Humanism appear in the late Middle Ages, especially through the efforts of the troubadours who focused on the beauty of nature and love, the role of the senses began to be appreciated more. It is one of the hallmarks of the fourteenth century, and the Renaissance, that it was beginning to be understood that the senses have a role in the formation of intelligence itself. Thus, even that old representative of the *ars antiqua*, Jacques de Liege, could admit, 'What is in the intellect was in the senses beforehand.'[4] Machaut symbolizes this nicely in a passage in which he points to the contribution of the senses to speech itself, which by its very nature is rational and not sensory.

> I summoned up all my senses together and then forced myself to speak ...
> 'My dear and revered lady, worthy of praise and honor, perfect in every quality heart can imagine, eyes see, ears hear, hand draw, mouth say ... taste savor, touch feel, desire or will or heart sense ...'[5]

On the other hand, Machaut acknowledges the central belief of earlier philosophers in stating that of our various faculties, Reason must rule. In his 'Remede de Fortune,' for example, the character Hope contends that Reason must still rule, even over states like happiness.[6] Happiness here perhaps is meant in the context of the result of moral behavior, for in another poem Machaut defines the determination of good and bad as the chief concern of Reason, who says,

> For goodness I give my reward,
> But badness earns severe reproof
> For I am judge of everything.[7]

Similarly, in 'The Judgment of the King of Navarre,' where Machaut himself is a character in the poem, there are introduced a number of allegorical characters including Temperance, Peace, Harmony, Faith (escorted by Constancy), Charity, Honesty, Prudence (who carried Wisdom in her heart), Generosity (who sees nothing) and Sufficiency. Here Machaut points out again that Reason must also rule over the senses:

---

4 Jacques de Liege, 'Speculum Musicae,' quoted in F. Joseph Smith, 'Ars Nova—A Re-Definition?' in *Musica Disciplina*, XVIII (1964), 34.

5 Guillaume de Machaut, 'Remede de Fortune,' trans. James Wimsatt and William Kibler (Athens: The University of Georgia Press, 1988), 294.

6 Ibid., 304–306.

7 Guillaume de Machaut, 'The Tale of the Alerion,' trans. Minnette Gaudet and Constance Hieatt (Toronto: University of Toronto Press, 1994), lines 4403ff.

> Just then Reason took charge of me
> So that afterward in her keeping she had
> My heart, my senses, and my thoughts,
> And thus they could resist
> And struggle against false ideas.[8]

In Machaut's 'Le Jugement du roy de Behaigne,' a similar group of allegorical figures appear in the castle of the King of Bohemia, including Sincerity, Honor, Courtesy, Beauty, Desire, Cheerful Happiness, Bravery, Valor, Love, Loyalty, Generosity, Will, Thought, Wealth, and Youth, followed by the observation, 'and then Reason who was mistress over all.'

> Et puiz Raison, qui de tous fu maistresse.[9]

We are relieved when Machaut allows one allegorical character to disagree. When the debate is over love and its consequences, Loyalty stipulates, 'A lover would be a fool to listen to you, Reason.'[10] This no doubt reflects a common observation: no matter how much you want to believe that Reason rules our actions, the ordinary experience of love proves otherwise. Nothing demonstrates this more clearly than speech. In complimenting good speech, Machaut describes it as 'moderate, well-chosen, and appropriate, based wholly on Reason.'[11] But, what happens to Reason-dominated speech when Love is present? It can, Machaut observes, force one,

> to cut short his words and interrupt them with sighs, drawn from the depths of his being, that render him mute and silent, and he has no choice but to remain speechless.

In fact, concludes Machaut, when it comes to expressing love, speech seems to be beside the point.

> Do you think that an esteemed, intelligent, loyal and prudent lady would care for someone who implores her love with polished, deceitful words and who, in begging her, colors his speech to play the sage?[12]

Machaut also observed that strong emotions can also interfere with the senses and cause them to behave 'irrationally.' He introduces this idea in the context of a large group of singing birds, which is important because bird song is a frequent metaphor in early literature for the most beautiful music.

---

[8] Guillaume de Machaut, 'The Judgment of the King of Navarre,' trans. Barton Palmer (New York: Garland Publishing, 1988), lines 1155ff.

[9] Guillaume de Machaut, 'Le Jugement du roy de Behaigne,' trans. James Wimsatt and William Kibler (Athens: The University of Georgia Press, 1988), 160.

[10] Ibid., 154.

[11] 'Remede de Fortune,' 180.

[12] Ibid., 262.

> And in more than thirty thousand places the birds, wide-throated, were trying to out-sing one another, as if it were a contest, making the whole orchard ring; and it's no lie that prior to Hope's visiting me in my need, my senses had been so distorted that I'd not noticed the birds or their music, or how merry they all were. But this should not be held against me, because there are two things that falsify the senses and cause them to react irrationally: these are great joy and great sadness.[13]

Today, hopefully, we have learned to give both the rational and experiential sides of ourselves equal merit and we might simply say that the emotions speak for a different side of us. Machaut, in another poem, seems to reflect this in a passage which reminds us of an old popular song, 'Your lips say "No," but your eyes say "Yes."'

> Thus she subjects him to reproach
> That she speaks to him with her mouth:
> Yet when she utters this aloud,
> A sweet glance says the opposite.[14]

These comments by Machaut about the sharp distinction between the rational and the experiential are clearly related to a popular philosophical topic of this period, the relationship between pleasure and pain. Mauchaut ponders this in the most vivid language. First a lady speaks of the joy of love:

> In him were my hope and my joy, my pleasure, my heart, my love, my thoughts and my desires. My heart could enjoy every good simply by seeing and hearing him. He was my every consolation; he was my every pleasure, my every solace, my joy, my treasure.[15]

He then paints an equally vivid picture of the pain which can follow joy.

> Alas! Unhappy me! Now all's reversed, for my pleasures have become grief-filled toils and my joys are bitter grief; my thoughts, which once brought consolation to my heart and comforted it sweetly in its sorrows, are and will always be painful, sad, and bitter.

Machaut joins in the opinion of much ancient literature in observing that when it comes to love, its very definition is a blending of pleasure and pain.

> Thus I felt many wounds, at one moment sweet, at another bitter, at one pleasant, at another disagreeable, at one sad, at another joyful. For the heart that feels Love's wound is not always in one mood, nor sure of joy or tribulation; rather, it is subject to the whims of the fortune of Love. But with head hung like a bear, I accepted her sweet biddings, whether for joy or for sorrow, meekly like a perfect lover, loyal in word and in deed.[16]

---

[13] Ibid., 334.

[14] 'The Tale of the Alerion,' lines 371ff.

[15] 'Le Jugement du roy de Behaigne,' 66ff.

[16] 'Remede de Fortune,' 188. Machaut returns to this theme in 'The Tale of the Alerion,' lines 1010ff and 1465ff.

In another place he points out that the lessons love teaches man are not of the nature of 'discipline, rules, order or Reason.'[17] Rather, he says, he has learned from his own *experience*, and not otherwise, that,

> the heart of a lover who loves deeply is now joyful, now mournful, now laughing, now crying, now singing, now lamenting, now happy in its plaint, now trembling, now sweating, now hot, now cold.

One of the by-products of the societal pressures which brought an end to the 'Dark Ages' was the birth of the modern universities. By the Renaissance they, and no longer the church, were rapidly becoming the center for debate. It followed that secular education began to have new recognition during the Renaissance. In this regard, we think the most interesting discussion of education by Machaut is his description of the ideal student, in particular the skills and attitudes the student must have. It is especially interesting that he observes that education must begin at an early age, before the student acquires too much experience. And when he speaks of the importance of honoring and serving one's profession, and that learning is easily forgotten if not put into practice, we cannot help but feel that some of these thoughts were with the music student in mind.

> He who wishes to learn any skill must take heed of twelve things: first, he must choose something to which his heart most leads him and for which he has a natural inclination, because a person does not willingly finish what he seeks to do contrary to his will, since Nature stands against him. He should love his master and his profession above everything; and he must honor, obey, and serve them; and he must not feel he is enslaving himself, for if he loves them, they will love him; and if he hates them, they will hate him; he can gain nothing otherwise. He must receive instruction meekly; and he must be careful to follow it, for learning is difficult to retain and easily forgotten when it is not put into practice. He should be diligent, assiduous, and eager for knowledge, for thus can he attain wisdom. And he should seek it at an early age, before his heart turns to wickedness through too much experience; for the true state of innocence is like the white and polished tablet that is ready to receive the exact image of whatever one wishes to portray or paint upon it. And it is also like wax that can be written upon, and which retains the form and imprint exactly as one has imprinted it. Truly it is the same with human understanding, which is ready to receive whatever one wishes and can apprehend whatever one sets it to: arms, love, other arts [*autre art*] or letters. For there is nothing so difficult that it cannot master it if it so chooses, providing it is willing to work and toil in accordance with what I have said above.[18]

Nothing is more characteristic of fourteenth-century thought than a new emphasis on the importance of feeling in music, therefore it is no surprise to find in Machaut, as a purpose of music, the very modern idea that music can express what nothing else can.

---

[17] Ibid., 214ff.

[18] 'Remede de Fortune,' 168ff.

> So I decided that I would compose, according to my feelings towards you and in praise of you, a lai, a *complainte*, or original song; for I did not dare or know how to tell you otherwise how I felt, and it seemed to be better to tell in my new song what was oppressing and wringing my heart than to try by some other method.[19]

For the composer of art music, this feeling is inseparable from the inspiration to compose. Thus Machaut confides, 'you alone who inspired my song, rhyme, and joyful subject.'[20] Similarly when Machaut is 'on trial' in 'The Judgment of the King of Navarre,' for his writings against women, the Lady says of his poetry,

> You know if you did good therein or wrong,
> Since you put your heart into them.[21]

And where such feelings are genuine, music becomes a form of Truth, Truth, moreover, which cannot be hidden.

> And if it please you, my dear lady, to consider the last little song I sang, of which I composed both words and music, you can easily tell whether I'm lying or speaking the truth.[22]

This is a very fundamental aesthetic principle, for in general the right hemisphere of the brain, which contains our feelings and the experiential aspects of music, cannot lie, in the normal sense of the word—because it cannot write or speak. The left hemisphere, the intellectual, speaking and writing side of us, as everyone knows can, and does, lie!

> Indeed my replies were very far from what I was thinking, for I constantly made white black.[23]

Machaut returns to this idea in 'The Judgment of the King of Navarre':

> The words you've uttered here
> Are nothing but frivolity.
> They are pretty to mouth in private,
> But they contain no substance.[24]

Machaut also mentions one of the most traditional purposes of music, to express joy.

> And for the joy I felt I composed this rondelet as I went along.[25]

---

19 Ibid., 368.

20 Ibid., 376.

21 'The Judgment of the King of Navarre,' lines 875–876.

22 'Remede de Fortune,' 374.

23 Ibid., 386.

24 'The Judgment of the King of Navarre,' lines 3988ff.

25 'Remede de Fortune,' 398.

Similarly,

> So I went along singing and so happy in my song …[26]

This, and the closely related purpose, to solace the listener, were obviously among the most important purposes of music for Machaut. In the Prologue to his collected works which he made at the end of his life, Machaut dwells on this at length. First, he promises the allegorical figure of Love not to write anything sad or difficult to understand, but only pleasant and sweet works which will soften and nourish hardened hearts.[27] He says he can bear witness to this from his own experience, for when he is in this joyous state, his only thought is the making of an appropriate poem or song.[28] Even if his subject is sad, the poet's manner must be gay, for a heart full of sadness cannot sing gaily. The melancholy man, on the other hand, is to be censured, nor could he possibly create anything so pretty. The very nature of music, says Machaut, requires the artist-lover to be joyful. 'Music is a science which asks that one laugh, and sing, and dance. It does not care for melancholy, nor for the man who is melancholy.'

> Et Musique est une science
> qui vuet qu'on rie et chante et dance.
> Cure n'a de merencolie
> Ne d'homme qui merencolie.[29]

Again, in 'The Tale of the Alerion,' Machaut observes that 'melancholy is a condition of no value.'[30]

'Wherever Music is, she makes men rejoice.' In the closing section of the Prologue, Machaut says this is his mission: music and poetry are meant to enlighten and soothe troubled mankind, as one can see in the example of David and his harp and Orpheus. We find the same philosophy mentioned in a letter to his lover, Peronnelle, where Machaut tells her, 'Singing is born of a cheerful heart, and tears come from sadness.' And in the 'Remede de Fortune,'

> I'll sing you a balladelle in my limpid voice, with new words and music, which you'll carry off with you, singing it to cheer up your heart as you go along, if it's troubled by any concern.[31]

In only one place does Machaut admit that music fails to solace. Although he is speaking of the music of birds, he echoes the thirteenth-century troubadours who often voiced the thought that even music cannot cheer the sad lover.

---

26   Ibid., 338.
27   Prologue, IV, 21ff.
28   Ibid., IV, 36ff.
29   Ibid., IV, 85ff.
30   'The Tale of the Alerion,' lines 3764.
31   'Remede de Fortune,' 326.

> I went there this morning to listen to their beautiful service and their merry singing, although my heart, which nothing can console, could take little pleasure in them.[32]

Machaut's student, Eustache Deschamps, speaks of the purpose of music renewing the spirit in terms of the poor tired scholar!

> Music is the final, and the medicinal science of the seven [liberal] arts; for when the heart and spirit of those applied to the other arts ... are wearied and vexed with their labors, Music, by the sweetness of her science and the melodiousness of her voice, sings them her delectable and pleasant melodies with her six notes in thirds, fifths, and octaves. These she performs sometimes with *orgues* and *chalumeaux* by blowing with the mouth and touching with the fingers; otherwise with the *harpe*, *rebebe*, *vielle*, *douaine*, with the noise of *tabours*, with *fleuthes*, and other musical instruments, so much so that by her delectable melody the hearts and minds of those who were fatigued, weighed down, and troubled with the said arts by thought, imagination or labor are revived and restored. Thus they are afterwards more able to study and labor with the other six arts.[33]

In the writings of Machaut we find the first composer of the Christian Era who speaks at length of his compositional process. The entire discussion is, at the same time, a statement of his personal philosophy with regard to the aesthetics of music.

In his famous Prologue, Machaut first meets the allegorical figure of Nature. Here he is not only associating his art with Nature in the Greek sense, but he is making the point that Nature supplied his inspiration.

> I, Nature, by whom all things take form,
> All that there is above and on earth and in the sea,
> Have come to you, Guillaume, a man I have formed
> For my part, in order for you to create
> Some new and pleasant love poems.[34]

With regard to inspiration, in Machaut's *Voir Dit*, his 'true story,' he speaks of this subject in several of his letters to his lover, Peronnelle. He tells her his work is often interrupted by the demands of his noble patrons, but more important if he does not hear from her, he stops working for lack of inspiration.[35] But if he is inspired he says he can write one hundred lines a day.[36]

However, composition requires more than inspiration, it also requires skill. Therefore Nature loans Machaut her three children, Reason [*sense*], who will make him clever; Rhetoric, who will instruct him in meter and rhyme; and Music, which will give him many, various and

---

[32] 'Le Jugement du roy de Behaigne,' 136.

[33] Eustache Deschamps, 'L'Art de Dictier,' quoted in Christopher Page, 'Machaut's 'Pupil' Deschamps on the Performance of Music,' *Early Music* 5, no. 4 (1977): 488ff, doi: 10.1093/earlyj/5.4.484

[34] Prologue, I, 1ff.

[35] Quoted in *Le Livre du Voir-Dit de Guillaume de Machaut* (Paris: Paulin Paris, 1875), 262 and 342.

[36] Ibid., 202.

pleasing songs.³⁷ 'Thus,' Nature says, 'you cannot fail at all.'³⁸ Here, in part, is a reference to having skill sufficient for 'correctness,' clearly another virtue of aesthetics in music. Nature promises, 'your works will be more renowned than those of any other because there will be nothing in them to criticize, and thus they will be loved by everyone.'³⁹ We can see how important the aspect of his technique was to Machaut in a remark he makes in 'The Remede de Fortune' regarding a poet and his work.

> I dared not refuse her, but rather read it from beginning to end, with trembling heart and bowed head, fearing there might be some mistake, since I had composed it.⁴⁰

Before leaving the subject of Nature, we should mention that Machaut attributes the power of music in part to the fact that all musical instruments are formed according to her laws, and her works are more perfectly proportioned than any others.

> Tous ses fais plus a point mesure
> Que ne fait nulle autre measure.⁴¹

But in addition to inspiration and skill, experience is also necessary to art. This is provided to Machaut by another allegorical figure, Love, who offers her three children, Sweet Thought, Pleasure, and Hope. It should also not escape our attention that Love (experience) is not introduced to Machaut by Nature, but rather she comes independently. Love promises that from her children 'you can derive great assistance, and this will help you invent and compose many a pretty poem about them.'⁴² Machaut responds that Love and her children have 'greatly clarified for me the themes I have to treat.'⁴³

Thus it is with the combination of skill and experience that Machaut is promised the necessary ability to compose 'tales and songs, double hoquets, pleasant lais, motets, rondeaux and virelais, complaints, ballades, in honor and praise of all ladies.'⁴⁴

But there is another requirement for composition which was clearly of the greatest importance to Machaut. The composer's work must come from the most genuine, heart-felt feelings. In a letter to Peronnelle, he explains, 'There is nothing so just and true as experience … He who does not create out of real feeling, counterfeits his words and songs.'

> Qui de sentement ne fait, Son dit et son chant contrefait.⁴⁵

---

37 Prologue, I, 10ff.
38 Ibid., I, 17.
39 Ibid., I, 19ff.
40 'Remede de Fortune,' 206.
41 Prologue, I, 99ff.
42 Ibid., III, 17ff.
43 Ibid., IV, 13ff.
44 Ibid., II, 12ff.
45 'Le Livre du Voir-Dit,' 61.

Machaut returns to this stipulation again in his poem 'Remede de Fortune.'

> And since I was not always in one mood, I learned to compose chansons and lais, ballades, rondeaux, virelais, and songs, according to my feelings, about love and nothing else; because he who does not compose according to his feelings falsifies his work and his song.[46]

> [Et pour ce que n'estoie mie
> Tousdis en un point, m'estudie
> Mis en faire chansons et lays,
> Baladez, rondeaus, virelays,
> Et chans, selonc mon sentement,
> Amoureus et non autrement;
> Car qui de sentement ne fait,
> Son oeuvre et son chant contrefait.]

The character in this same poem now composes a lai to express his feelings [*fait un lay de son sentement*]. Among the words for this song, one finds Machaut once more stressing the acceptance of varied emotions of love.

> And if I experience any sorrow
> from Desire, I don't complain,
> for her sweet laughing eye
> completely soothes
> the sorrow born of Desire.[47]

At the end of the song, Machaut once again returns to feeling.

> But I composed it to her praise in accord with the skill I possessed, and as near to my feelings as I well could.[48]

We gain some insight into what 'feeling' meant to Machaut in the following passage. While the thirteenth-century troubadour also mentioned the pain of love, one does not find in that literature the emphasis on the feelings themselves that we read here—it is a distinction of the Renaissance.

> Then, like one accustomed to sighing, I uttered a lament and sigh from the depths of my heart, accompanied by weeping and washed in tears; and with great effort I turned toward her my flushed, pale, sad, sorrowful, and weeping face, full of suffering. But I said nothing to her because I was unable to speak; instead, I gazed fixedly at her.[49]

---

[46] 'Remede de Fortune,' 188.

[47] Ibid., 196.

[48] Ibid., 206.

[49] Ibid., 254.

Finally, in another letter to Peronnelle, Machaut reveals one more important vital characteristic of the good composer—one must always double-check one's work!

> My sweetheart, I have composed the rondel which contains your name and I would have sent it by this messenger; but by my soul, I have never listened to it and I am not accustomed to sending off anything I compose before I have listened to it.[50]

In all early literature the most conspicuous hallmark of art music, as compared to functional or entertainment music, is the presence of the contemplative listener, one who is actively listening to the music. When one considers how strongly Machaut emphasizes the importance of genuine, deeply felt feelings on the part of the composer, it is no surprise that we find him concentrating on the receiving end of those feelings—the listener—to a degree that is almost entirely missing in Medieval literature. Nowhere in Medieval literature do we find a composer so fervently interested in the reaction of the listener as we do in Machaut's 'Remede de Fortune.'

> How do you like it? What do you say? ... What do you think of my song? ... What do you say? ... Won't you tell me if I sing well or poorly?[51]

Later in this same poem a listener is described.

> When she had finished her ballade, which was very pleasant and agreeable to my ears and in my heart, since I'd never before heard such sweet harmony, I was overjoyed. But if the sweet music pleased me, the words brought me more joy than anyone could conceive. So I made a great effort to learn it, and memorized it so quickly that before she'd left the place or had even finished singing it, I knew both the words and the music.[52]

Machaut's 'Le Jugement du roy de Behaigne' begins with an allusion to the 'sweet' singing of birds, a topic found in so much literature in the thirteenth and fourteenth centuries, but here the observer not only really seems to be listening to one, but takes pleasure as a listener.

> I dropped gently to the ground and hid myself as best I could beneath the trees, so it could not see me there, to listen to the very sweet melody of its delightful song. And I took more pleasure in listening to its sweet singing that ever I could tell.[53]

---

[50] 'Le Livre du Voir-Dit,' 258.

[51] 'Remede de Fortune,' 280.

[52] Ibid., 328ff.

[53] 'Le Jugement du roy de Behaigne,' 60.

Since contemplative *listening* to the music is one of the essential aspects of what we mean by 'concert' music, we have often pointed out in these essays that the brief concert *after* the dinner, as opposed to dinner music, is one of the earliest forms of concerts in the modern use of the word. And there is no reason to doubt that these nobles were informed listeners. Christine de Pisan wrote of the fourteenth-century French King Charles V,

> The King understood so well every aspect of music, which is the science of harmonizing sounds by slow and fast notes ... that no discord could pass unperceived by him.[54]

Machaut, in his 'Remede de Fortune,' describes one of these after dinner concerts, not only making the point that the musicians appear after the dinner, but he even suggests that they arrive dressed for a concert, as it were. We should also mention here that, just as it was an artistic challenge for painters to portray one of each possible instrument in similar canvases, the poets loved to list one of each instrument. We should not believe such an ensemble really played together.

> And after the meal you should have seen the musicians arrive, all combed and comfortably attired. They played various harmonies, for there all in a circle I saw vielle, rebec, guitar, lute, Moorish guitar, small psaltery, cittern, and the psaltery, harp, tabor, trumpets, nakers, portative organs, more than ten pairs of horns, bagpipes, flutes, musettes, douaines, cymbals, bells, timbrels, the Bohemian flute and the large German cornett, willow flutes, a fife, pipe, Alsatian reed pipe, small trumpet, busines, psaltery, a monochord (which has a single string), and a straw pipe all together. And it certainly seemed to me that such a melodious sound had never been perceived or heard; because I heard and perceived each one of them, according to the pitch of his instrument—vielle, guitar, cittern, harp, trumpet, horn, flute, pipe, bladder pipe, bagpipe, naker, tabor, and whatever could be played with finger, pick or bow—performing in perfect harmony there in the little park.[55]

It is also interesting to note that after this post-dinner concert concluded, instruments were made available for the guests to play as part of their own entertainment. And, no doubt as an obvious compliment to the aristocrats, Machaut mentions both their ability to read from the page and to improvise and attributes to them knowledge of both *ars antiqua* and *ars nova* styles.

> After they had performed an estampie, the ladies and their company went off by twos and threes, holding hands, to a very beautiful room; and there all the men and women alike who wanted to relax, dance, sing, or play at backgammon, chess or parsons found all they needed at hand and ready for games, singing, and music [*par notes, ou par sons*]. And there were musicians more skilled and knowledgeable in both the new and old styles.[56]

---

[54] Christine de Pisan, *Le Livre des Fais et Bonnes Meurs du Sage Roy Charles V*, ed. S. Solente (Paris, 1936) II, 34.
[55] 'Remede de Fortune,' 390ff.
[56] Ibid., 392.

In another poem, 'La Prise d'Alexandrie,' Machaut describes the events surrounding a visit of the King of Cyprus to Prague. The castle there was 'paradise on earth. There they had all instruments,' among which Machaut lists no fewer than thirty-five. The visiting king, listening to this performance, 'marveled very much and said that in his life he had never experienced such great melody.'[57]

One continues to find much poetry and love song in fourteenth-century France which is reminiscent of the troubadour repertoire of the previous century. A poem by Jean Froissart, singing the praises of a lady, is a perfect example.

> I will serve my lady always,
> For truly I cannot spend
> My time or youth
> In any better way.
> And so with happy heart,
> Awaiting her desire,
> Most joyously
> I will sing both night and day.[58]

Similarly, in the Prologue to his collected works, Machaut has Love warn him,

> But above all else, take care that you are not emboldened
> To write anything full of disrespect,
> And never slander any of my ladies.
> Rather in every case you are to praise and exalt them.
> Know well that if you do otherwise,
> I will most cruelly take away your standing.
> Instead, do everything in honor and thus advance yourself.[59]

It is in the context of the frequency of this theme that 'The Judgment of the King of Navarre,' by Machaut, is understood. In his poem, at the end of Machaut's 'trial' for having written unkindly about women, he is given the following sentence:

> You must—the thing is certain—
> Compose a lay for the first,
> And agreeably, without resisting;
> For the second, a song
> Of three stanzas and a refrain
> —Listen how I qualify this—
> A song which begins with the refrain
> Just like the ones sung at a dance;
> And for the third, a ballade.
> Now don't act like you're sick about this,

---

57 Guillaume de Machaut, *La Prise d'Alexandre*, ed. L. de Mas Latrie (Geneva, 1877), 69.
58 'Lay 4,' in Kristen Figg, *The Short Lyric Poems of Jean Froissart* (New York: Garland Publishing, 1994), 59.
59 Prologue, III, 21.

> But respond happily,
> As we have commanded.[60]

It is also enlightening that Machaut stipulates these love songs might also be appropriately performed as instrument works.

> By God, it is a long time since I have made such a good thing to my taste; and the melodies [*tenures*] are as gentle as fine pap. Whoever performs it on organs, bagpipes, or other instruments, that is its proper nature![61]

It is surely another clue to art music, when Machaut says here that he has composed these love song 'to my taste.' That others heard this repertoire as art music is reflected by Deschamps' comment, after the death of Machaut, that his death will be mourned by princes and kings because 'his song gave much pleasure to nobles, ladies, and bourgeois.'[62] And Deschamps said of Machaut,

> O flower of the very flowers of melody itself,
> So sweet master of such great talent,
> O Guillaume the earthly god of harmony.

As for the value Machaut himself placed on these love songs, we have his comments in letters written to his lover, Peronnelle. He tells her not to circulate copies of what he sends her, for he is thinking of making music for them,[63] and he says that some nobles who have learned of their affair have requested copies.[64]

In view of the fact that Machaut's education was that which might ordinarily lead to the priesthood, it is somewhat surprising that he so rarely refers to the music of the Church. One passage is particularly interesting, however, where he describes a group of flagellants and their music, a bizarre form of religious piety stemming from the thirteenth century, but which continued in Bohemia during the 1340s.

> At this time a company arose
> At the urging of Hypocrisy, their lady,
> Who beat themselves with whips
> And crucified themselves flat on the ground,
> While singing to an instrument
> Some new song or other,
> And according to them, they were worth more
> Than any saint in Paradise.
> But the Church attended to them,

---

[60] 'The Judgment of the King of Navarre,' lines 4181ff.

[61] 'Le Livre du Voir-Dit,' 69.

[62] Guillaume de Machaut, *Oeuvres*, ed. Ernest Hoepffner (Paris, 1908–21), I, iiiff.

[63] 'Le Livre du Voir-Dit,' Letter VI.

[64] Ibid., Letter XXV.

> Forbidding them to beat themselves,
> And likewise condemned their song,
> Which little children were singing,
> And excommunicated all of them
> By the power God had granted it,
> Because their self-abuse
> And their song were heresy.[65]

Dinner music was a common form of functional music and a horn or trumpet signal for the guest to wash their hands was the first announcement for dinner in a castle. Here we read 'the horns sounded the call to wash, and the loud trumpets too.'

> Et il estoit prez heure de souper.
> Et a ce mot on prist l'yaue a corner
> Par le chastel, et forment a tromper.[66]

This signal which calls the guest to dinner is frequently mentioned in literature of the Renaissance and Baroque. But since this literature is nearly always concerned with the aristocracy, we almost never read of what this signal means to the servants. Machaut's words are so vivid it seems as if we really are standing watching.

> When Mass was over, I heard a chamberlain sounding a trumpet loudly. You should have seen all the servants! Each hurried to his station, one toward the pantry, another to the wine cellar, the others to the kitchen, according to what each prepared. Messengers and stable boys set up benches, trestles, and tables. It was quite a sight to see them hurrying to and fro, bringing rushes, spreading rugs, shouting, hollering, and sweeping—it was bedlam to hear them call to one another in French, Breton, German, Italian, English, Occitan and Norman, and in many other unusual languages. It was a marvel to see elsewhere the carvers arranging, polishing, decorating, and straightening things, readying the water, slicing bread for their masters, preparing the plates, calling for tablecloths, removing cheeseskins with their own hands, one sitting down, the other scurrying along, yet another scrubbing off dirt, others washing and cleaning their hands, one more and the other less, before going to sit down. They were making quite a racket, with everyone shouting and exclaiming: 'Hurry up! Mass is ended and they've sounded the trumpets for dinner long since!'[67]

---

[65] 'The Judgment of the King of Navarre,' lines 241ff.
[66] 'Le Jugement du roy de Behaigne,' 160.
[67] 'Remede de Fortune,' 388.

Francesco Petrarch on Music

FRANCESCO PETRARCH (1304–1374) was one of the first of the important humanists. Born to the family of a very successful lawyer, he enjoyed the advantages of the best available education, including the study of law at the universities of Montpellier and Bologna. But he found he could not follow the law profession, for he had concluded that to be successful one must 'practice dishonestly.'[1]

Petrarch's attention turned to reading the works of the ancient Greek and Roman writers and while still in his early twenties developed into an important classical scholar. He became a man obsessed with the past, begging friends to look for lost titles he had come across in his readings, discovering manuscript works of Cicero in a library in Verona and even writing letters addressed to Homer and Cicero. After 1330, when he joined the service of Cardinal Colonna, he was able to continue his studies with few other obligations.

Most of his hundreds of poems deal with Laura, a woman whom history cannot identify. Other than his declaration that he met her in church on Easter Sunday, 1327, there is little proof she actually existed. But his poetry, much of it in the spirit of the thirteenth-century troubadours, made him famous and he was rewarded by his coronation as poet laureate in Rome in 1341. This decade saw many of his friends, including his lover, Laura, and his son, killed by a great plague known as the Black Death. In 1350 he met Boccaccio, with whom he enjoyed a close personal and professional relationship for the rest of his life.

In 1337 he purchased a small house at Vaucluse, near Avignon, where like an early Rousseau he began to extol the virtues of Nature. But it was not Romanticism that he helped introduce to the fourteenth century, but Humanism and the Renaissance.

Petrarch's reading of the ancient Greek and Roman classics stimulated his interest in philosophy, a pursuit he knew had little appeal to the average person.

> 'Philosophy, you go poor and naked!' says the mob, bent on low gain.[2]

Aside from this distance from the public which Petrarch felt, there was a certain pessimism which also runs through much of his writing. One can see an example of this in a general comment about the mind.

> Nature has provided for all other living creatures the wonderful remedy of a certain ignorance. Only man has memory, intellect and foresight ... which he turns to his ruin and suffering.[3]

---

[1] Letter to Boccaccio, quoted in James Robinson, *Petrarch, The First modern Scholar and Man of Letters* (New York: Putnam, 1914), 67.

[2] 'La gola e 'l sonno et l'oziose piume,' in *Petrarch's Lyric Poems*, trans. Robert Durling (Cambridge: Harvard University Press, 1976), 42.

[3] 'Remedies for Fortune Fair and Foul,' trans. Conrad Rawski (Bloomington: Indiana University Press, 1991), I, Preface, 1.

While he recognized the contribution of the senses and personal experience, Petrarch's roots as a Catholic helped cause him to believe the old dogma that Reason must dominate. In his 'Remedies for Fortune Fair and Foul,' Reason speaks for itself.

> SORROW: My mind is rent into conflicting parts.
> REASON: The philosophers divide the mind into three parts, the first of which they place at the very top, as if in a citadel, that is, in the head. This is the ruler of human life, heavenly, serene, and always close to God, where tranquil, decent intentions dwell. The second part is located in the chest, where anger and malice boil; the third, in the lower parts which house lust and desire.[4]

In the Preface to this same book, he states this even more strongly.

> You should read the book *as if* those four most famous, twin-born passions of the mind, HOPE or DESIRE and JOY, FEAR and SORROW, brought forth at the same time by the two sisters Prosperity and Adversity, fiercely assaulted from all sides the mind of man, and REASON, who governs this citadel, took on all of them at once. In her buckler and helmet, by stratagem and proper force, and, more so, with God's help, she fends off the weapons of the roaring enemies around her.[5]

Higher education meant, to Petrarch, the traditional seven Liberal Arts, which still included music. For the extent of these studies he had a clear respect.

> Life is too short for any of the [liberal] arts ... To know completely but one art in all its respects has never been accomplished even by the most outstanding scholars.[6]

Petrarch probably felt that such extensive development of the mind was probably not possible for the common man, which led him to this definition of a good mind: 'If it serves liberal studies it is a precious instrument; if not, it is ponderous, perilous and laborious.'[7]

Thus, in his 'Remedies,' he makes it clear that he believed that attempts to educate the general public were largely a waste of time.

> SORROW: It was my lot to get an unteachable pupil.
> REASON: You are tilling barren soil! Unhitch your oxen—why torture yourself? Quit bothering him and yourself. There are so many needed and inevitable chores; it is sheer stupidity to look for useless ones!
> SORROW: I have a pupil who cannot be taught how to pursue the study of letters.
> REASON: If he can be taught to pursue virtue, urge him to do that: and you will have enriched him with the best of all the arts. But if he cannot do either, leave him alone, lest you try pouring into a leaky jug water, which will not stay in it, and exhaust yourself in continual weariness.[8]

......

---

[4] Ibid., II, lxxv, 171.

[5] Ibid., I, Preface, 10.

[6] Ibid., I, xlvi, 149–150.

[7] Ibid., I, vii, 23.

[8] Ibid., II, xli, 103.

> Teach those who can be taught, do not bother with those who cannot learn, and avoid tiring them as well as yourself. Art rarely overcomes nature.[9]

It follows that Petrarch seemed to have little respect for the teacher whose duty it was to attempt this futile public education. In this same passage he makes a surprising reference to the value of the liberal arts.

> Let them teach who can do nothing better, whose qualities are laborious application, sluggishness of mind, muddiness of intellect, prosiness of imagination, chill of the blood, patience to bear the body's labors, contempt of glory, avidity for petty gains, indifference to boredom … What is more, neither grammar nor any of the seven liberal arts is worth a noble spirit's attention throughout life. They are means, not ends.[10]

Petrarch reflects on the extent of his own early education in his little biographical essay addressed to posterity.

> I learned as much of grammar, logic, and rhetoric as my age permitted, or rather, as much as it is customary to teach in school: how little that is, dear reader, thou knowest.[11]

Petrarch also shared with earlier Church philosophers the idea that of the emotions, love was the one which most interfered with rational stability.

> Love, I transgress and I see my transgression, but I act like a man
> who burns with a fire in his breast; for the pain still grows, and
> my reason fails and is almost overcome by my sufferings.[12]
> ......
> If to love another more than oneself—if to be always sighing and
> weeping, feeding on sorrow and anger and trouble—
> If to burn from afar and freeze close by—if these are the causes
> that I untune [*distempre*] myself with love, yours will be the blame,
> Lady, mine the loss.[13]

Petrarch also reflects traditional medieval thought, that one cannot comfortably enjoy pleasure for it so easily turns into pain. In one of his poems, he complains, 'thus my singing is converted to weeping.'[14] We find this same thought again in his 'Remedies.'

> JOY: I delight in song and the music of stringed instruments.

---

9   Ibid., I, lxxxi, 223.
10 Letter to Zanobi da Strada, in *Letters from Petrarch*, trans. Morris Bishop (Bloomington: Indiana University Press, 1966), 108.
11 Quoted in Robinson, *Petrarch, The First modern Scholar and Man of Letters*, 66.
12 'Amor, io fallo et veggio il mio fallire,' in *Petrarch's Lyric Poems*, 394.
13 'S' una fede amorosa, un cor non finto,' in Ibid., 380.
14 'Mia benigna fortuna e 'l viver lieto,' in Ibid., 526.

> REASON: Ah, how much better to delight in tears and sighs. For weeping that ends in joy is preferable to joy that ends in sorrow.[15]
>
> ......
>
> Sorrow is the closest neighbor to earthly delights.[16]

Much in the spirit of the thirteenth-century troubadours, Petrarch warns that love is more often pain than pleasure.

> I never wish to sing again as I used to, for I was not understood, wherefore I was scorned, and one can be miserable in a pleasant place.[17]

Being a poet and singer much in the mold of the thirteenth-century troubadours, we are not surprised that Petrarch's writing on Beauty is centered first in the beauty of woman. While his attraction to this form of beauty is documented in his poetry, there was a part of him which was reserved. It was another manifestation of the problem which concerned him with regard to the emotions distracting Reason. He seemed to distrust the idea that Beauty alone was a virtue, rather one must find an additional virtue. In his 'Remedies,' Petrarch quotes from a letter by the Roman Prince, Domitian, 'Be assured that nothing is more pleasing than beauty, but nothing shorter-lived.'[18] Later in this same work, Petrarch recasts Domitian's observation in his own words:

> There is nothing more fleeting than beauty, especially a woman's. Remember: He who loves his wife because of her beauty will soon hate her.[19]

Where then, does one find virtue in Beauty? Petrarch quotes Seneca as saying, 'worth is more pleasing in a form that's fair,' then objects that this is wrong because it suggests only the eye of the beholder makes the judgment. 'Worth,' instead should be a matter of the value inherent in the thing itself.[20] Subtle is better, adds Petrarch, for 'hidden beauty is sweetest.'[21] Petrarch does not explore this question much further, preferring to evade the issue by declaring that the mind is more beautiful than the body.

> For the beauty of the mind is much sweeter and longer lasting than that of the body, and it too has its laws regarding the beautiful and the ordering of parts.[22]

---

15 'Remedies,' I, xxiii, 70.

16 Ibid., I, liv, 168.

17 'Mai non vo' piu cantar,' in *Petrarch's Lyric Poems*, 208.

18 Ibid., I, ii, 16ff.

19 Ibid., I, lxvi, 194.

20 Ibid., I, ii, 18.

21 'Mai non vo' piu cantar,' in *Petrarch's Lyric Poems*, 210.

22 'Remedies,' I, ii, 18.

Regarding the aesthetic purpose of Art, Petrarch provides the most familiar definition, that it is to delight.

> All earthly things have been made to be subordinate to man. Some to feed him, some to clothe him, some to carry him, others to protect him, others yet to train and teach him, and remind him of his place—some also to delight him and to revive his spirits when his affairs have tired him.[23]

Petrarch makes an interesting observation, here presumably about music: it is possible for art to delight the observer, even if the observer does not know why. In this regard he quotes from his favorite philosopher, Cicero.

> … it merely tickles their ears, without their knowing why, but cannot penetrate their thick heads, because the avenues of intelligence are obstructed.[24]

That this happens is part of what we call Universality in art. The artist understands what communicates universally, without the necessity of the observer knowing anything about the actual details of the craft of the art. Thus, Cicero's comment reminds us of an almost identical one by Mozart,

> … these passages are written in such a way that the less learned cannot fail to be pleased, though without knowing why.[25]

One discovers originality by looking inward, reflecting on one's own experience. Petrarch adds, 'Experience makes art, says Aristotle. All the arts prove his statement.'[26]

Petrarch also addresses the very important aesthetic question of the obligation of the artist to the public, or the audience. It was immediately clear to him that for an artist to have the goal of pleasing the audience was wrong.

> It's idiocy to regulate our lives not according to intelligent reason but to suit popular fads … To follow the fashions of the vulgar mob, whose manners we laugh at and whose lives and opinions we despise, is to be more idiotic than the mob.[27]
>
> ……
>
> Experience, the great teacher, is on my side, though the silly, unteachable mob is against me.[28]

Probably Petrarch felt this was an impossible goal to begin with, for he wondered, 'How can I please all? I have always striven to please only the few.'[29]

---

[23] Ibid., II, xc, 211.

[24] Letter to Boccaccio, in Robinson, *Petrarch, The First modern Scholar and Man of Letters*, 184.

[25] Letter to his father, December 28, 1782.

[26] Letter to Francesco Bruni, in Robinson, *Petrarch, The First modern Scholar and Man of Letters*, 228.

[27] Letter to his brother, Gherardo, in Ibid., 92.

[28] Letter to Laelius, in Ibid., 159.

[29] Letter to 'Socrates,' in Ibid., 18.

The artist who purposely desires to please the general audience usually does so for the purpose of money. Here, Petrarch exempts the highest artist.

> If anyone says that craftsmen are not seeking fame but money, I would probably have to agree as far as the common sort is concerned. But I deny it regarding the very best craftsmen. There are many indications of this—the way they persist in their efforts, regardless of the time they spend and the material losses they suffer. They even spurn cash lest they impair their fame.[30]
>
> ......
>
> Money, certainly, does not appeal at least to noble minds as a worthy reward of study. It is for the mechanical trades to strive for lucre; the higher arts have a more generous end in view.[31]

Petrarch also makes some interesting observations on several of the individual arts, which we might introduce with his belief that one should restrict oneself to only one discipline.

> No one intellect should ever strive for distinction in more than one pursuit. Those who boast of preeminence in many arts are either divinely endowed or utterly shameless or simply mad.[32]

Regarding painting, Petrarch found that this art was widely treasured during the fourteenth century—but for the wrong reasons. Not only had paintings become a status symbol, but Petrarch, following the ancient Church dogma that man should not love art but rather He that made the artist, was concerned that a man might like them *too* much, admiration turning to devotion.

> JOY: Paintings delight me.
> REASON: An inane delight ... A remarkable unsoundness of the human mind—to admire anything, save itself, although among all the works, not only of art, but also of nature, there is nothing more admirable ...
> JOY: Paintings delight me more than anything.
> REASON: You take delight in the pencil strokes and colors which please because of price and skillfulness—their variety and artistic composition. And you are fascinated by the lifelike gestures, the movement in these inanimate and immobile pictures, the faces jutting out of posts, and the portraits that seem about to breathe and make you think that they might utter words. The danger here lies in the fact that great minds, in particular, are captivated by these things—and what a peasant will pass off with brief enjoyment, a man of intellect may continue to venerate with sighs of admiration. This is a complicated matter, and our task here is not to inquire into the origins of art and its development, nor the wonders of its works, the dedication of the artists, the mad extravagance of princes, and the enormity of the prices which brought paintings from far across the oceans to Rome and hung them in the temples of the gods, the bedrooms of the emperors, on public avenues, and in galleries. Nor was this sufficient. The Romans themselves had to apply their right hands, as well as their minds, which should have been applied to greater tasks, to the pursuit of painting ...

---

30 'Remedies,' II, lxxxviii, 204.

31 Letter to Tomasso da Messina, quoted in Robinson, *Petrarch, The First modern Scholar and Man of Letters*, 221.

32 Letter to Giovanni Andrea di Bologna, quoted in Ibid., 286.

Thus, when these fictions and contours in feckless colors delight you too much, turn your eyes to Him, who painted feelings on the face of man, intellect on man's mind, the stars on the heavens, the flowers on the earth—and you will disdain the paintings you admired.[33]

Sculpture, because of its additional dimension, Petrarch found to be a higher art to the extent that it was closer to nature. Here again, however, he was disturbed by the fact that this art had become 'popular.'

>JOY: But I enjoy statues.
>REASON: A different art, but the same madness—and there is but one origin and one purpose of all the arts, though there are various materials ... Sculpture is nearer to nature than painting. Pictures appeal much to the eye, but sculptures can be touched, feel substantial and solid, and are of durable body. This is the reason why no paintings by the ancients survive today, but countless statues ...
>
>There is one of those arts in which the human hand imitates nature, called *plasticen*—the plastic art. It works with plaster, wax, and retentive white clay and is, perhaps, the most attractive among all related arts—closer to virtue or, at least, less hostile to moderation and frugality, which suggest that images of gods and men be made of simple clay rather than gold ...
>
>Once, statues were the hallmarks of virtue; now, they are attractions for the eyes. Once, they were erected in honor of great accomplishments ... Today, priceless statues of foreign marble are erected unto rich merchants.
>
>JOY: Artistic statues give me pleasure.
>REASON: Nearly any kind of material admits artistic treatment. I understand that in all things your pleasure is brought about by noble skill joined with noble materials ...
>
>The enjoyment of talent, engaged in with moderation, is acceptable—enjoyment, particularly of those who excel in it, because, if envy does not hinder you, it is easy to admire in another what one loves in oneself.[34]

Petrarch's views on the theater are as hostile as those of the early Church fathers and for the same reasons, the bad influence on the character of the observer and for the inherent lack of Truth.

>JOY: I enjoy all kinds of spectacles.
>REASON: The circus or the theater, perhaps—two places notoriously inimical to decent conduct. Even a bad person who goes there returns worse. This path is unknown to good people, and if they follow it because of ignorance, they risk contagion ...
>
>A performance which is neither rendered nor viewed with honesty; nor is it easy to say whether the actor is more infamous or the spectator, the stage more than the audience—unless we acknowledge the fact that men are drawn to the former often by poverty, but to the latter by ostentation.[35]

Although himself one of the great poets of the fourteenth century, Petrarch seems to have developed a disdain for his own art, again in part because it had become too popular. Too many common people had begun to write poetry and to think of themselves as poets.

---

33 'Remedies,' I, xl, 125ff. It is also interesting here that Petrarch correctly identifies that it is the entire face which expresses emotions. Most early writers mistakenly believed that it was only the eyes.

34 Ibid., I, xli, 130ff.

35 Ibid., I, xxx, 90ff.

> Poetry, a divine gift granted to few, has fallen into the hands of the mob; I shan't go so far as to say it is profaned and prostituted.[36]

He attributes this popularity to poetry's superficial pleasure, whereas its great virtue, appealing to deep meditation, was possible only by a superior mind. In a letter to Pierre d'Auvergne, Petrarch again complains that so many common people are trying to write poetry, quoting Horace, 'Lettered and unlettered, we all write poems all the time.'

> Need I dwell on minor excesses? Carpenters, cloth-fullers, farmers abandon their plows and the tools of their trades to prate on the Muses and Apollo. One can't imagine how far has spread this plague, which used to afflict only a few. If you ask why, I should answer that poetry is very sweet to the taste, but it is to be appreciated by only a few superior minds possessing a lofty, incurious contempt for common concerns, given to high meditations, and with an appropriate natural gift …
> I live in distress, and I hardly dare to appear in public, for these cranks pop up from everywhere. They interrogate me, they snatch at me, they instruct me, they dispute, they quarrel.[37]

Petrarch's reaction was to once again separate himself from what he refers to as 'the mob,' and turn his attention to spiritual literature.

> I think that the Muses and Apollo will not merely grant me permission, they will applaud, that after giving my youth to studies proper to that age, I should devote my riper years to more important matters.[38]

It is a particular disappointment in reading the works of this thoughtful man, to find that he speaks so rarely of music—even though he was a musician, a singer of his own poetry and, as we know from a letter in which he mentions 'those sweet sounds I used to draw from my lute.'[39] Even in a letter to the French composer, Philippe de Vitry, Petrarch extols the beauties of the Italian countryside, but says nothing of Italian music.[40] It may be that his taste in music was for the 'old-fashioned' styles, for in a letter to Boccaccio, while no doubt thinking primarily of literature, Petrarch's words sound very much like the criticism which the members of the *ars antiqua* of this period were leveling at de Vitry and his *ars nova* colleagues.

> O inglorious age! that scorns antiquity, its mother, to whom it owes every noble art,—that dares to declare itself not only equal but superior to the glorious past.[41]

Regarding the aesthetic purpose of music, Petrarch, as we see in his own poems, gives as its chief virtue the ability to soothe.

---

[36] Letter to Francesco Nelli, in *Letters from Petrarch*, 115ff.
[37] Letter to Pierre d'Auvergne, in Ibid., 120ff.
[38] Letter to Francesco Nelli, in Ibid., 190.
[39] Letter to Giovanni Colonna, in *Letters from Petrarch*, 35. In his will Petrarch bequeathed his lute to the impresario Bombasi.
[40] Letter to Philippe de Vitry, in Ibid., 86ff.
[41] Letter to Boccaccio, quoted in Robinson, *Petrarch, The First modern Scholar and Man of Letters*, 208.

It is right and just that I sing and be joyful.
It is just that at some time I sing, since I have sighed for so long a
time that I shall never begin soon enough to make my smiling
equal to so many sorrows.[42]

......

Therefore if at any time I laugh or sing, I do it because I have no
way except this one to hide my anguished weeping.[43]

Nevertheless, for the listener, Petrarch finds a hidden danger in this capacity of music.

JOY: I am charmed by songs and sounds.
REASON: Also wild animals and birds are tricked by song. More remarkable yet, even the fish are touched by the sweetness of music ... Not believed but known by experience is the fact that, daily, man deceives man with smooth words and, to be short, that there is nothing more suited to deceit than the voice.
JOY: I am soothed by pleasant music.
REASON: And so, they say, soothes the spider before it bites. And the physician anoints before he cuts. And the fouler, and a woman, both cajole whom they want to deceive. And the murderer embraces whom he will kill and the octopus whom he will drown. And some of the worst men are to be feared all the more when they are most gentle in manner and voice, which we read in particular of Prince Domitian. Hardly any kind of soothing is beyond suspicion.[44]

......

JOY: I shall not weep. I shall sing and cheer myself with poetry, as lovers do.
REASON: I must admit that this special folly of lovers is one of the most remarkable things—not only confined to the vulgar crowd, whose habit to find any madness excusable has become their second nature, but also affecting men of the highest culture among them the Greeks and Romans. Thus we know that the poets of Greece and your own country have written brilliantly, some about the loves of others, most about their own, and have earned fame for their eloquence although they deserved notoriety for their conduct ...

Yet, when it comes to what you call 'cheering yourself' in this malady, which you imagine to be done by poetry, let Horace's little poem and its query serve as my answer:

> *Do you suppose that with verses such as these,*
> *sorrow and passion and the burden of care can*
> *be lifted from your breast?*

By talking and singing love is strengthened and inflamed, not extinguished or relieved; and the songs and poems which you utter do not heal, but irritate the wound.[45]

---

42 'Lasso me, ch' I' non so in qual parte pieghi,' in *Durling, Op. cit.*, 150.

43 'Cesare, poi che 'l traditor d'Egitto,' in Ibid., 204.

44 'Remedies,' I, xxiii, 70.

45 Ibid., I, lxix, 202ff.

In his fourth pastoral *Eclogue*, however, Petrarch returns to the traditional praise of the ability of music to provide solace, as he patriotically comes to the defense of Italy in a debate between Gallus (France) and Tyrrhenus (Italy) as to whom the gift of poetic expression belongs. Petrarch declares the god Daedalus first makes a gift of music to Tyrrhenus and one of its primary purposes is to provide solace.

> *Tyrrhenus*: Bearing his lyre he drew near me. 'Take this, my lad,' so he bade me; 'Let it console your cares and beguile your long days of labor.'

Gallus desires to possess the virtues of music, represented by the lyre, and says,

> GALLUS: Fix yourself the price you would take for that little
>   Object, and high though it be I'll pay—and add something to it.
> TYRRHENUS: So for this 'little' thing you'd pay a great price? Nay, you know not
>   What it is worth or you'd call it a great thing. In troubles it soothes us,
>   Raises our weary spirits, affords our friends consolation,
>   Rids our heart of their sorrows, making them once more joyful,
>   Dries up our tears and appeases all our complaints and even
>   Banishes fear, brings hope to our hearts and calm to our faces.[46]

So effective is this capacity of music, that it provides him the courage to face the trials of the world.

> TYRRHENUS: Nay my wealth is my lyre. By its virtue alone I am free of
>   Fortune's incessant onslaughts and poverty—all of the fetters
>   Fastened on me by the world. With my music I traverse full often
>   Wasteland and woods and ascend barren crags and fearlessly wander
>   Through the dark silence of night, while the birds and the caverns applaud me.
>   All of my cares, as I sing, fall away and are lost in the shadows.[47]

Petrarch also acknowledges that one of the powerful attributes of music is its power to *move* the minds of men.

> JOY: Song moves me.
> REASON: But to what purpose? Without doubt music has great power over the noble hearts of men. But its effects are various beyond belief. And, to omit what is of no concern, it moves some to shallow mirth, others to pure and devout joy and, sometimes, even to pious tears. This variety has led many great minds to different conclusions. Athanasius, as everybody knows, forbade the use of singing in the churches to ward off vanity. Ambrose, eager to kindle active devotion, decreed that they should sing. Augustine states truthfully in his *Confessions* that he allowed both views and that it was difficult for him to settle his doubts in this manner.[48]

---

[46] *Petrarch's Bucolicum Carmen*, trans. Thomas Bergin (New Haven: Yale University Press, 1974), IV, 22, 41ff.
[47] Ibid., IV, 56ff.
[48] 'Remedies,' I, xxiii, 71.

This power of music he finds, in his third pastoral *Eclogue*, can even work its magic on the 'stern and tenacious mind.'

> And tell how their voices blending
> Sang one harmonious song as they danced, each one in her circle,
> Hymning the spirit of mankind in all of its various motions,
> Whence comes our love of sweet fame, our cultivation of music,
> Joy in the use of our minds, be it wit or the stern and tenacious
> Cult of the intellect; aye and thereto the sources of rapture,
> Righteous judgment, and art in discerning the will of the heavens,
> Power to charm our hearers.[49]

Petrarch finds that sometimes this characteristic of music can have a disturbing effect.

> Song, you do not quiet me, rather you inflame me to tell of what steals me away from myself.[50]

Observing this power of music no doubt made Petrarch take special notice of the fact that the ancient philosophers emphasized the influence of music on character development. He mentions this in a passage in which he has been praising the music of angels and of heaven.

> Right now you relegate the judgment of the sounds to a deaf sense, which so far some may still regard as a small matter, although it has troubled great men. Nor was it without cause that Plato, a man of divine intellect, considered music as pertaining to the state and the improvement of moral conduct in the commonwealth.[51]

In another place Petrarch mentions, almost with a sense of surprise, the esteem for music held by the ancients. Here, he concedes that appreciating music represents a measure of refinement, but, as in the case of painting and sculpture, he cautions once again against the listener being *too* involved.

> JOY: It is pleasant to sing.
> REASON: What gives you pleasure now once gave pleasure to the Greeks. Among them anyone who could not sing or play instruments was considered ignorant. This, Cicero writes, happened to Themistocles of Athens, the most illustrious of the Greeks, when he refused to play the lyre at banquets ... It is amazing that a Socrates should in his old age devote his efforts to the harp. But it should not surprise us that Alcibiades was made to study the [aulos] by his uncle Pericles, because this was regarded as most worthy by the ancients and, in fact, was even taught among the liberal arts ...
>
> In the present age such an ardent zeal for music has as yet not come to possess the mind of every prince, but it has taken possession of the hearts of a few, particularly the worst ones. For Caligula was extremely fond of singing and dancing. As for Nero, it is unbelievable how much he was devoted to the study of the kithara and what pains he took with his voice. But it is stupid and utterly ridiculous when in the very night that was the last one of his life ... he should grievously bewail again and again

---

49 *Petrarch's Bucolicum Carmen*, III, 112ff.
50 'Perchee la vita e breve,' in *Petrarch's Lyric Poems*, 160.
51 'Remedies,' I, xxiii, 73.

the downfall, not of such a great prince, but of such a great musician. I omit others. Even today, in your own age, we find here and there that pleasure of the ear which to enjoy honestly and soberly constitutes a measure of humane refinement. Yet to be overwhelmed and voluptuously possessed by it is nothing but sheer foolishness.[52]

In one curious passage, Petrarch, the important early Italian humanist, lapses back into the old medieval Scholastic concept of music being an expression of mathematics. As a musician himself, how could he make this nonsensical statement?

> A deaf person can know the tones and numbers characterizing the intervals of fifth and octave, as well as the other proportions of the musical scale with which musicians work. Although one does not hear the sounds of the human voice, of strings or the organ, he nevertheless may understand in his mind their fundamental canon and, doubtless, will prefer the intellectual pleasure to a mere titillation of the ear.[53]

Petrarch makes a few interesting observations about performance. First, speaking of rhetoric, no doubt with echoes of his legal studies, he emphasizes that content cannot be equated with eloquence. Today, thinking of music, we might say, you can't judge the music by the performance.

> Sweetness and elegance—I do not know how alluring or deceptive they are, but they do not imply anything noble or truthful. Before just judges the sweet and flowery pleading of a dishonest man matters no more than the makeup of a streetwalker.[54]

Regarding performance in general, he returns again to his belief that, above all, one must not have the audience foremost in mind.

> No way is more prone to error or leads more directly to the brink of disaster, than the steps of the multitude. Almost everything which the crowd praises deserves to be condemned.[55]

Among those in his poems to whom he joins an association with music, we find,
Plato:
> There stood the painter and gymnast and, in adolescence, the singer,
> And in his age a traveler and a diviner....[56]

......

Varro:
> Another told of the sea-gods and how they put into our music
> Strange, esoteric matters.[57]

......

---

[52] Ibid., I, xxiii, 71ff.

[53] Ibid., II, xcvii, 241.

[54] Ibid., I, ix, 27.

[55] Ibid., I, xi, 32.

[56] Ibid., X, 142.

[57] Ibid., X, 195. Not all modern scholars agree whom Petrarch is thinking of in this fascinating reference.

Terence:
> I heard a foreign born slave, to whom a fair prison had given
> Freedom at last and moreover endowed with a marvelous talent,
> Sing of the manners of men and their tricks and their wiles, of the secret
> Fears of uneasy old age and of youth and its sport and the guileful
> Arts of procurers. He used an Italian [plectrum] for his verses,
> Having long since forgotten his native African patois.[58]
>
> ......

And, *Virgil:*
> Truly a kingly shepherd he governed he fields and the woodlands,
> Second in song to none, had he but the leisure for singing.[59]

From these earlier artists, Petrarch learned also that hard work and practice is necessary even for the modest results he attributed to his own music.

> Saw too a race of melodious singers, all of them masters,
> Content to stand under its shade and fashion the rarest of garlands.
> And on that greensward I too have learned—for much avails practice
> Long and laborious—how to vary my notes, singing many
> Albeit modest songs, and have dared to crown my own temples
> Finally with that same leafage.[60]

Once again, considering Petrarch himself played the lute, we are disappointed that he makes almost no specific reference to the performance of art music which he actually heard. Only in the most indirect references can one surmise that such activity existed. For example, in a letter scolding his son, Petrarch mentions in passing, 'at a harmonious concert who hates the lute?'[61] In another place, referring to finding comfort in the sounds of nature, Petrarch says even the nocturnal noises of frogs might be imagined as 'the sweet consort of viols.'[62]

In a letter to an old university friend, Petrarch, mentions that in Bologna, music was experiencing the same decline he had mentioned regarding the arts in general. In speaking of the choral-dance performances, he mentions that songs have been replaced with laments and 'girls dancing in chorus' by gangs of bandits.[63]

---

[58] Ibid., X, 232.
[59] Ibid., X, 289.
[60] Ibid., X, 366ff.
[61] Letter to his son, Giovanni, in *Letters from Petrarch*, 184.
[62] 'Remedies,' Op. cit., II, xc, 213.
[63] Letter to Guido Sette, in *Letters from Petrarch*, 266.

One of the chief descriptors of art music which we have looked for is the appearance of the contemplative listener. In Petrarch it is in his pastoral settings which he describes such listeners. In the first of his *Eclogues*, for example, which deals with the relative virtues of the monastic life versus the literary life, a listener hears music which stirs and moves his soul.[64] And later, in the same Eclogue,

> Here, in the depths of night, you will see a shepherd tuning
> Notes of unrivaled sweetness, to make you in time forgetful,
> Headless of all other matters. And surely you cannot call idle
> Music which now can arouse you, now hold you fixed and enraptured.[65]

Similarly, in one of his poems, the listener is moved by the singing of birds.

> And from its shade came forth such sweet songs of divers birds
> and so much other delight that it had rapt me from the world.[66]

Because they are inspired, serious and have real listeners, we consider love songs in the style of the troubadours as also being art music. Much of Petrarch's poetry is in this style. As Durling points out, 'Petrarch's wide familiarity with troubadour poetry is evident on every page.'[67] These were real art songs, yet they are scarcely mentioned in general music history texts. They were an expression of the humanists interest in the ancient Greek model and a fifteenth-century authority credits Petrarch himself for reviving this form.

> Those forms of poetry usually are numbered which consist of eight lines [*strambotti*] or three lines [*elegies*], which type Francesco Petrarch is said to have first established among us as he sang his exalted poems with a lute.[68]

There is no doubt that much poetry in the fourteenth century was still sung in performance. A note in Petrarch's own hand in the margin of his copy of his *Canzoniere* reads,

> I must make these two verses over again, singing them and I must transpose them: 3 o'clock in the morning, October the nineteenth.[69]

---

[64] 'Ecologue I,' lines 20ff.

[65] *Petrarch's Bucolicum Carmen*, I, 54ff.

[66] 'Standomi un giorno solo a la fenestra,' in *Petrarch's Lyric Poems*, 502.

[67] Ibid., 9.

[68] Cortesi, 'De Cardinalatu,' quoted in John D'Amico, *Renaissance Humanism in Papal Rome* (Baltimore: Johns Hopkins University Press, 1983), 106.

[69] Quoted in John Larner, *Culture and Society in Italy, 1290–1420* (New York: Scribner's, 1971), 163.

Additional confirmation that this poetry was sung are found in poems which begin such as 'Io canterei d'Amor' (I would sing of love).[70] Others associate verses and 'notes':

> For the last need, O wretched soul,
> mobilize all your wit, all your power,
> while we still have the breath of life.
> There is nothing in the world that cannot be done by verses;
> they know how to enchant asps with their notes,
> not to speak of adorning the frost with new flowers.
>
> Now the meadows are laughing with new grass and flowers:
> it cannot be that her angelic soul
> will be deaf to the sound of the amorous notes;
> if our cruel fortune has greater power,
> weeping and singing our verses … [*cantando i nostri versi*][71]

We have referred to his rejection of this repertoire in his later years. But once again, in this regard, it is interesting that in a letter to his brother he refers to the poems as songs, as he recalls 'our silly songs, full of false and indecent praise of loose women.'[72]

Art music must be inspired, a point which Petrarch also makes in his love poetry. Indeed, in the second of these, he maintains that if he fails, it will be for lack of inspiration, not craft.

> Song, one of your sisters has gone before, and I feel the other
> in the same dwelling making herself ready, wherefore I rule
> more paper.[73]

Petrarch also mentions the quality of the performance, with regard to this repertoire. In his third *Eclogue*, which is a pastoral allegorical tale of his pursuit of Laura, the shepherd turns to music as the means of gaining the love of the girl, only to discover his ability is not sufficient.

> Indeed I have bent every effort,
> Hoping my song would avail me; I knew that you were responsive
> Sooner to notes of the Muse than the jingle of gold. At first, though,
> Doubts began to assail me, concerning the road I had chosen:
> Only hoarse sounds emerged from my pipe.[74]

After practicing before goats and bees, and aided by the god Argus, he improves.

---

70 Also And I go singing, in 'Per mezz' i boschi inospiti et selvaggi'; I sang, now I weep, in 'Cantai, or piango; et non men di dolcezza'; I wept, now I sing, in 'I' piansi, or canto; che 'l celeste lume'; I went singng of you many years, in 'Alma felice che sovente torni'; and I dared, singing, to complain of Love, in 'Mentre che 'l cor dagli amorosi vermi.'

71 'La ver l'aurora, che si dolce l'aura,' in Ibid., 400.

72 Letter to his brother, Gherardo, in *Letters from Petrarch*, 94.

73 'Gentil mia Donna, I' veggio,' in *Petrarch's Lyric Poems*, 166.

74 *Petrarch's Bucolicum Carmen*, III, 60ff.

Finally, in his tenth pastoral *Eclogue*, Petrarch pays tribute to the ancient Greek singers, the original lyric poets. In this passage he is thinking of Simonides, Stesichorus, Alcaeus, Sappho, Philetas of Kos, Antimachus of Colophon, Callimachus and Anacreon.

> There too stood a singer of sacred things and their priesthood, beside him
> One who glorified arms and the trumpets of war; the former
> Dear to the gods and the latter to men. And another was singing,
> Armed with a bow and lyre, of the captured wolf and the sheepfolds
> Spared in the Lesbian plains; so his song and his deeds won him honor.
> Among these great doctors of art stood a girl no less skilled than they are;
> Sweetly she sang of love and its snares and its burning anguish.
> Touching her rosy lips with a cinnamon flute she could often
> Move the bright stars above with her gentle and soft lamentations.
> Many admirers she has; one from Kos, widely known of his verses
> Praising his Bittis, and one, from Klaros, whose song was of Lyde,
> And the Cyrenian bard who was Africa's gift to the Nile and
> Likewise the shepherd of Teos consumed by a Samian fire.
> Nor do the lovers of our day esteem her less highly, adopting
> Her plaintive and humble accents, voiced in like varied measures.[75]

If the somber Petrarch has left so few descriptions of art music, it comes as no surprise that he barely mentions the lower aesthetic representatives. Considering the fact that he became absorbed with spiritual matters late in life, we might have expected some expression of interest in Church music. Certainly, the one comment he made, which is at all descriptive, makes us wish for more discussion. Only in his first *Eclogue* do we find this reference to Church singing, which he describes as 'deep reaching into souls with mysterious sweetness.'[76]

Ceremonial music is mentioned in Petrarch only in a passing reference to 'the trumpet blasts of soldiers,'[77] and in a description of a pastoral procession in his third *Eclogue*.

> Multitudes cheered as they marched 'midst the triumphant blare of the trumpets ...
> Hither came other singers, too many to mention, among them
> He of the threefold reed, your dearly cherished Parthenias.[78]

There are two references to occupational music, one of the 'plowmen singing in the fields'[79] the other of the 'poor hoer.'

---

[75] Ibid., X, 81ff.

[76] Ibid., I, 103.

[77] Letter to Giovanni Colonna, in *Letters from Petrarch*, 35.

[78] Bergin, Op. cit., III, 137, 156.

[79] Letter to Guido Sette, in *Letters from Petrarch*, 268.

> When the sun turns his flaming wheels to give place to night and the shadow descend more widely from the highest mountains, the poor hoer takes up his tools and with words and mountains tunes lightens his breast of all heaviness.[80]

In all the writings of Petrarch there is little enthusiasm to be found for the music of traditional entertainment. Even in the case of banquets, which are frequently mentioned in all early literature, one gathers the impression that Petrarch didn't have much fun, finding them ostentatious and boring, 'Trumpets blare and cymbals crash, and it seems that everything serves pomp and circumstance.'[81]

For those who had to make their living providing entertainment, Petrarch had little sympathy.

> One law holds for entertainers and parasites: both of them chase after the rich with alluring flatteries. For lowly hangers-on it is sufficient to fill their bellies. But entertainers, to whom the very mention of food is an insult, have to satisfy in other ways their greed, which is bottomless and everlasting.[82]

In another reference to this environment he places Entertainment Music above other forms of entertainment.

> A nobler amusement [than entertainers] is provided by well-modulated music, created, as you know, according to a certain liberal art—while the environment produced by entertainers appeals only to vanity and shamelessness.[83]

We conclude with Petrarch's attack on dancing, a form of entertainment for which he subscribes to the strong moral objections of the Church.

> JOY: I enjoy dancing.
> REASON: I would be surprised if the sound of stringed instruments and pipes did not suggest dancing to you, and, according to established rule, one vanity would not be followed by another greater and more disgraceful one. Because in song there is a certain sweetness, often profitable, even saintly. Yet dancing offers nothing but sensuous and worthless exhibition, hateful to decent eyes and unworthy of a man ...
>
> > [Imagine dancing without music playing] just the silly girls and their partners, softer than girls, turning around and prancing forward and backward in the silent room. Tell me, have you ever seen anything more absurd and inane? In reality, the ugly motions are, of course, accompanied by the sound of strings and pipes, as one mindless folly view with another one ...
> >
> > There is less immediate pleasure in dancing than anticipation of pleasure to come. Dancing is the foreplay of Venus: to lead around the simpering girls dazed by music, to touch them and squeeze them, and, under the guise of being sociable, fondle them. Licentious hands, licentious eyes, licen-

---

80 'Ne la stagion che 'l ciel rapido inchina,' in *Petrarch's Lyric Poems*, 116.
81 'Remedies,' I, xix, 55.
82 Ibid., I, xxviii, 85.
83 Ibid., I, xxviii, 84.

tious whisperings, the stamping feet, the dissonance of the singing and the blaring brasses, the to-and-fro of bodies ... all drive off restraint and modesty, they all arouse lechery and wanton indulgence ...

Since you are afflicted in this way ... as long as you cannot go without dancing altogether, indulge in it sparingly and with the utmost restraint; do not act in any way over dainty and like a woman, but let, at all times, manly rigor show itself, even beyond its usual limits ...

I cite Seneca ...

> Scipio would disport his triumphal and soldierly person to the sound of music, moving not with the voluptuous contortions that are now in fashion, when men even in walking squirm with more than a woman's voluptuousness, but in the manly style in which men in the days of old were wont to dance during the times of sport and festival, risking no loss of dignity even if their own enemies looked on.[84]

---

[84] Ibid., I, xxiv, 73ff.

Giovanni Boccaccio on Music

GIOVANNI BOCCACCIO (1313–1375), reared in Florence and Naples, was destined by his family for a career in finance, but like his great friend, Petrarch, he abandoned his profession for poetry.

> If my father had only been favorable to such a course at a time of life when I was more adaptable, I do not doubt that I should have taken my place among poets of fame. But while he tried to bend my mind first into business and next into a lucrative profession, it came to pass that I turned out neither a business man nor a lawyer, and missed being a good poet besides.[1]

Today, of course, we recognize him as a famous poet after all. Like Petrarch, much of his poetry was inspired by a woman he could not have, whom he also met in church on an Easter Sunday. In this case, at least, we know she was a real person, Maria d'Aquino, a natural daughter to King Robert of Naples. Boccaccio called her Fiammetta (little flame) and dedicated many of his large works to her, including *Filocopo*, *Teseide* (the basis of Chaucer's 'The Knight's Tale') and the *Amorosa Visione*.

She appears as well as a character in his masterpiece, one of the supreme masterpieces of all literature, *The Decameron*. There is no greater testimonial to the new spirit of Humanism than the fact that Boccaccio could write this work, so filled with joy, humor, beauty and the zest for living, in the wake of the great plague, the Black Death.

Again like Petrarch, Boccaccio became obsessed with ancient literature, saving works from oblivion and promoting them. Upon the ominous urging of a dying cleric, Boccaccio returned to religion late in life and contemplated selling all his books and becoming a monk and a letter from Petrarch helped prevent the destruction of his writings. He died in poverty and, indeed, when Petrarch died the previous year he left in his will money to buy a mantle for Boccaccio. A biographical note written by an author born during Boccaccio's lifetime paints a rather unhappy portrait of his life.

> I will not write Boccaccio's biography at this time, not because he does not deserve greatest praise, but because I do not know the particulars of his birth or his personal condition and life. Without knowledge of such things, one should not write. However, his works and books are well known to me, and it is clear to me that he had a great mind and was extremely cultured and hardworking. It is amazing that he wrote so many things … He was greatly hindered by poverty, and was never content

---

[1] *Genealogia Deorum Gentilium*, XV, x, quoted in *Boccaccio on Poetry*, trans. Charles Osgood (New York: The Liberal Arts Press, 1956).

with his life; on the contrary he continually wrote complaints and moaned about himself. Sensitive and disdainful by nature, he had many problems because he could neither bear to be with his own peers, nor in the company of princes and lords.[2]

Like Petrarch, Boccaccio accepted without question the ancient dogma that Reason must govern man. It does seem odd for a poet, however, that Boccaccio wrote so little of the value of sensory information and experiences. In one passage, like an early Church father, he assigns Reason to man and the senses to animals.

> Animals show their feelings by a movement of their heads, by a whistle or a roar, but to man alone was it granted to express thoughts in words. Nor was this without cause; for how could nature in any other way more wisely separate mankind, endowed with a divine soul, from the beasts, controlled only by sensuality. Servants of their senses, the thoughts of the latter are only on earthly things, and they take pleasure only in these. For the beast it seems superfluous to have a tongue for easy speech. We conclude, and rightly, that unintelligent beings had far better exist without tongues.[3]

In the same spirit, in another place he warns of the dangers, not the virtues, of the senses.

> Since the eyes are the gates of the spirit, through them lust sends messages to the mind, through them love sighs and lights blind fires. Through them the heart sends sighs and shows its shameful affections. If one knew them well, he would either keep them closed or turn them heavenward or fix them upon the ground. No other ways but these are safe.[4]

Boccaccio's discussion of the emotions is limited to the poet's despair of love. He observes, following most early philosophers, that the stronger emotions, in particular love, have the negative effect of depriving one of Reason. In his *Corbaccio*, he cries out to the lover, 'Oh, poor fool! Where is the meager power of your reason (no, rather, the expulsion of your reason) leading you?'[5]

In a passage in his *Concerning Famous Women*, Boccaccio, sounding very much like a medieval Church father, argues at length on the dangers of love, how it enters through the senses and how lovers lack Reason. Boccaccio finds virtue only in the first stages of love, when it tends to improve a man's behavior—including the inspiration to study music.

> This must instill great fear in men who are solicitous of their well-being and must shake them out of their lethargy, when it is clear what a strong and powerful enemy threatens them. We must therefore be vigilant and arm our hearts with great strength, so that we are not overcome against our wishes. First a man must resist. He must curb his eyes so that they do not see vain things, close his ears like an asp, and tame lust with continual toil, because love seems alluring to men who are not wary, and at first sight it is pleasing. If it is well received, when it first enters it pleases a man with happy hopes,

---

[2] Leonardo Bruni (1369–1444), quoted in *The Decameron*, trans. Mark Musa and Peter Bondanella (New York: Norton, 1977), 188.

[3] 'Against the Detractors of Rhetoric,' in *The Fates of Illustrious Men*, trans. Louis Hall (New York: Ungar, 1965), 165.

[4] 'Medea,' in *Concerning Famous Women*, trans. Guido Guarino (New Brunswick: Rutgers University Press, 1963), 37.

[5] *The Corbaccio*, trans. Anthony Cassell (Urbana: University of Illinois Press, 1975), 2.

makes him adorn himself, encourages good behavior, *savoir-faire*, dances, songs, music, games, conviviality, and similar things. But after love through foolish consent has seized the entire man, conquered freedom, and chained and bound the mind and the fulfillment of desires is delayed beyond what had been hoped, it awakens sighs, forces the mind to make use of wiles without differentiating between vices and virtues as long as it achieves it desires, and it numbers among its enemies anything which is contrary to this ... If the lovers do not attain their desires, then love, lacking reason and using his spurs and whip, increases their worries, heightens desire, and brings almost intolerable pain, which cannot be cured by any remedy except tears, laments, and at times death.[6]

In his *Corbaccio*, we find an even more extensive catalog of the dangerous effects of Love.

> Love is a blinding passion of the spirit, a seducer of the intellect, which dulls or rather deprives one of memory, a dissipator of earthly wealth, a waster of bodily strength, the enemy of youth, and the death of old age, the parent of vices, and the inhabiter of inane breasts, a thing without reason or order, without the least stability, the vice of unhealthy minds, and the stifler of human liberty.[7]

In one place in *The Decameron*, Boccaccio reverses this thought and concludes that one must simply set aside the faculty of Reason before engaging in thoughts of Love. In the seventh story of the eighth day, we read,

> The learned scholar, laying aside philosophical speculations, turned all his thoughts to her.[8]

With respect to the ancient philosophical debate over the nature of pleasure and pain, Boccaccio finds that pleasure is an important component of the successful choice of a profession. One is by nature, he suggests, attracted to the profession in which he finds pleasure.

> While there is one kind of person, there are still many kinds of interests, and each person decides where he can achieve his own happiness as he wishes. For this reason a soldier chooses the wars, the lawyer the court, the farmer the fields—the examples can be infinite. The poet seeks out a solitary place and lives there. The soldier enjoys the tumult of battle, the lawyer enjoys the argumentation and litigation, the farmer the beauty and greenery of the fields, the poet the harmonious sound of verses. The first is accustomed to combat, the second to judgments, the third to the progress of the seasons, and the last to contemplation. To the soldier the final goal is victory, to the lawyer it is money, to the farmer it is harvest, and to the poet it is reputation. This arises from a great complexity of professions, though each has only one end. What pleases one person is justifiably unattractive to another.[9]

Boccaccio offers a final general warning regarding pleasure. One can never be content in pleasure, because Fortune can in a moment reverse it.

---

6 'Iole,' in *Concerning Famous Women*, 46ff.

7 *The Corbaccio*, 23.

8 *Decameron*, II, 589.

9 'The Author Acquitted and Poetry Commended,' in *The Fates of Illustrious Men*, 104ff.

> When your mind is filled with joy and something disturbs you, remember that you have risen by the same law as others and that you too will fall into insignificance and be punished for your offenses, if it so pleases Fortune. And so you are not deceived by any kind of belief in the stability of satisfaction, fix this in your mind: Whenever anyone's situation seems to be taken for granted by everturning Fortune, then in the midst of this unfortunate credulity, she is preparing a trap.[10]

Regarding the pleasures of love, Boccaccio joins nearly all early writers and philosophers in concluding that in the end there is more pain than pleasure resulting from the experience. Nowhere does he make this more personal than in the introduction to his *The Corbaccio*:

> I happened, as I had often done before, to begin thinking very hard about the vicissitudes of carnal love; and pondering over many past occurrences and musing to myself about every word and deed, I concluded that through no fault of mine I had been cruelly ill-treated by her whom I had chosen in my madness as my special lady and whom I honored and revered above all others and loved far more than life itself. Since it seemed to me that I had received abuse and insult in this affair without deserving it, after many sighs and lamentations, driven by resentment, I began not merely to weep bitterly but to cry out loud. I suffered so much, first bemoaning my stupidity, then the insolent cruelty of that woman, that by adding one grief to another in my thoughts, I decided that Death must be far easier to bear than such a life.[11]

In his dedication of *Theseus* to Fiammetta, however, he seems to find, through the memory of his lover, some solace for the pain of Love.

> Although departed joys which return to my memory in my present unhappiness are the unmistakable cause of heavy sorrow, it does not on that account displease me, O cruel lady, to revive in my weary soul from time to time the charming picture of your perfect loveliness … And its effect on me is the clearest proof that what I believe is true, because when the eyes of my mind behold it, a hidden sweetness, I know not how, beguiles my tormented heart, almost making it oblivious of its unremitting pains.[12]

Boccaccio seemed to be rather sensitive to criticism of poetry and in one place he categorizes some of the types of men who criticize poets and poetry. First, there are those 'madmen' who are simply arrogant and criticize everything in sight. Such men, Boccaccio finds, are usually uneducated in the subjects they profess to judge, thus his prescription for them:

> If they really are impelled by this desire for glory, and seek a reputation for wisdom, let them go to school, listen to teachers, pore over their books, study late, learn something, frequent the halls of brilliant debaters; and lest they rush into teaching with undue haste, let them remember the Pythagorean caveat, that no one who came to his school to speak on philosophical subjects should open his

---

[10] 'A Last Few Mourners and the End of the Book,' in Ibid., 242.

[11] *The Corbaccio*, 2.

[12] *Theseus*, trans. Bernadette McCoy (New York: Medieval Text Association, 1974), 335.

mouth until he had listened for five years. When they shall win praise in this respect, and earn genuine title, then, if they wish to come forward, let them lecture, or dispute, or refute, or inveigh, and vigorously press their opponents. But any other course is proof rather of madness than wisdom.[13]

Another who criticizes the poet is the lawyer, who, being interested only in money, cannot understand why anyone would desire a profession where they are destined to be poor. Boccaccio answers that the poet's reward is rather in wisdom and immortality.

> I readily grant therefore their contention, that poetry does not make money, and poets have always been poor—if they can be called poor who of their own accord have scorned wealth. But I do not concede that they were fools to follow the study of poetry, since I regard them as the wisest of men …
>
> ……
>
> Furthermore, if the privilege of long life is not granted a man in any other way, poetry, at any rate, through fame vouchsafes to her followers the lasting benefit of survival—rightly enough called a benefit, since we all long for it. It is perfectly clear that the songs of poets, like the name of the composer, are almost immortal. As for lawyers, they may shine for a little while in their gorgeous apparel, but their names in most cases perish with the body.[14]

Finally, Boccaccio, like Petrarch, did not associate himself with the broad public. In his dedication of his *Concerning Famous Women*, for example, he mentions that he wrote the work 'while away from the crude multitudes.'[15] In another book, he elaborates on his general distrust of the public.

> Envy tortures, but the multitude deceives. The first drives a man to destroy others; the second destroys him by his own conceit. The one inflames the mind; the other mocks hope … No one should ever put his faith in the praises of the common people. It is in the nature of the multitude to be ever changeable and perverse, preferring always conjecture to truth, crying always for activity, then deserting in times of danger. The crowd follows where Fortune goes, serves her humbly, but rules severely. And after bestowing its gifts, it kills those unfortunates who had trusted it.[16]

Boccaccio seems to stress, as the first aesthetic purpose of music, that it offer solace to the listener. At the end of the fourth day, in *The Decameron*, when customarily the group listens to one of its members sing a solo song, Phylostrato, the singer, is instructed,

> It is our pleasure that, so no more days than this one be troubled with your ill fortunes, that you sing such one thereof as most pleases you.[17]

---

13 *Genealogia Deorum Gentilium*, XIV, iiff.
14 Ibid., XIV, ivff.
15 *Concerning Famous Women*, xxxiii.
16 'Against the Faithlessness of the Common People,' in *The Fates of Illustrious Men*, 115ff.
17 *Decameron*, I, 364.

It is also most interesting that, when the song is finished, the narrator indirectly gives us another purpose of music, 'The words of this song clearly enough discovered the state of Phylostrato's mind.'

In the seventh story of the tenth day, a song intended to provide solace has quite a different effect.

> ... and then sang her sundry songs, the which were fire and flame to the girl's passion, whereas he thought to solace her.[18]

In the *Filostrato*, a kind of testimonial to medieval courtly love, a character is sent music for the specific reason of lifting his spirits.

> They immediately sent messages to their ladies that each of them should go and visit him and make entertainment for him with melodies and singers, so that he should forget his irksome life.[19]

Finally, in the romantic epic, *Theseus*, two disappointed lovers sing for their own comfort.

> Then, when she left, they returned to their earlier madness and often composed measured verse [songs] to comfort themselves in singing of her high worth. In this way they took some delight in their misfortune.[20]

Another potential purpose of music is to fuel the flames of love. In his *Amorous Fiammetta*, Boccaccio wonders who is immune to this influence of music?

> There the cool Sea banks and most pleasant gardens, and every other place besides, with divers feasts, with new devised sports, with most fine and curious dancing, with all kinds of amorous songs and [canzonets], made, played and sung by those lusty youths and sweet Nymphs, did resound forth marvelous and pleasant Echoes. Who is he therefore that can, amongst so many enticing pleasures there, keep himself free from Cupid?[21]

There was an element of this purpose of music which Boccaccio clearly disapproved of. In describing an early Roman woman, he mentions that 'with dancing and singing, which are instruments of sensuality, she turned to wantonness.'[22]

But, on the other hand, Boccaccio finds a virtue in the power of love for encouraging the study of music for the refinement of manners. In *The Decameron*, in the first story of the fifth day, we are given of list of the accomplishments necessary to turn a young man into a gentleman. Here we find he must learn to both sing and play an instrument ('song and sound').

---

[18] Ibid., II, 737.
[19] *Filostrato*, vii, 83, here trans. Nathaniel Griffin and Arthur Myrick (New York: Bilbo and Tannen, 1967), 469.
[20] *Theseus*, III, 38.
[21] *Amorous Fiammetta*, trans. Edward Hutton (Westport: Greenwood Press, 1926), 157.
[22] 'The Roman Sempronia,' in *Concerning Famous Women*, 173.

> Then, consorting with young men of condition and learning the fashions and carriage that befitted gentlemen and especially lovers, he first, to the utmost wonderment of everyone, in a very brief space of time, not only learned the first elements of letters, but became very eminent among the students of philosophy, and after ... he not only reduced his rude and rustical manner of speech to seemliness and civility, but became a past master of song and sound and exceedingly expert and doughty in riding and martial exercises, both by land and by sea.[23]

The purpose of music which we would regard as most important today is to communicate feeling. We know that what the common listener responds to in music is not the music itself, which would require everyone to be educated in music to appreciate it, but the communication of feelings. Boccaccio mentions this with regard to a love song.

> Love, heed not what my voice sings, but rather how much my heart, your subject, is filled with desire.[24]

In another place, Boccaccio turns this around and writes of the power of music to recreate feelings.

> And ... giving a willing ear to the skillful music, and the silver sounds of those instruments, which with passing sweet notes entered deeply into my mind, and, thinking of my Panphilus, I did at one time cover and hide, discord, feasts and grief because, listening to the pleasant noise made, every demi-dead spirit of love did regain their former vigor and force in me again: and the remembrance of those merry times did return again to my mind, in which the heavenly harmony of these instruments, touched with rare skill, was wont in presence of my Panphilus to work divers commendable and sweet effects.[25]

One passage suggests that Boccaccio would have agreed that aesthetic music must be inspired.

> Now let the Muse who concerns me most compose her verses through me. Let her now sing through me.[26]

In contrast to Petrarch, there is much in Boccaccio which offers clues to actual performances of music he must have heard. Sometimes he displays a knowledge of music by using it in analogy, as in his *Genealogy of the Gods*, when he mentions in passing the tuning of the harp and the variety of tones which make up an interesting melody.[27] But his works also contain numerous references to actual songs, and often with the lyrics as well, sung by various characters. In one place he even mentions the enjoyment of music by those rowing on the water.

---

23   *Decameron*, I, 371.
24   *L'Ameto*, 40.
25   *Amorous Fiammetta*, 161.
26   *Theseus*, VIII, 2.
27   *Genealogia Deorum Gentilium*, XV, x.

> We ploughed the gentle waves of the calm Sea, singing sometimes, and with playing sometimes on divers Instruments, went rowing up and down.[28]

Although once Boccaccio describes a song as 'ingenious,'[29] usually such music is described as 'sweet,' the term used in ancient lyric poetry to denote the most pleasing music. In the pastoral romance, *L'Ameto*, for example, the 'sweet voice of a ringing bagpipe' played by a shepherd, 'reached [the women's] ears.'

> So, moved by the pleas of the women, Teogapen put his mouth to the pierced reed, and entreated by them, following upon the music, he began to sing.[30]

Soon after, Boccaccio gives a more complete description of this musician as he accompanies another singer.

> Thus, giving full breath to the waxed pipe with swollen throat and riotous cheeks, he resolved it into sound with quick fingers which now opened and now closed the holes, making pleasant music; and with gestures he commanded that Acaten respond to Alceste, who began by singing his verses.[31]

A particularly interesting reference to art music is found at the beginning of his *The Decameron*, where Boccaccio gives a detailed account of the great plague under which so much of Italy suffered in the middle of the fourteenth century. In describing the different strategies by which people tried to avoid the plague, he mentions that some shut themselves up, eating only the most delicate meats and the finest wines 'they abode with music' and other diversions. This we take to be the private performance of art music, in contrast to a description of what must surely be popular music performed by those of an alternate lifestyle, those who 'carouse and make merry and go about singing and frolicking.'[32]

Throughout ancient literature, one finds descriptions of banquets where music is heard after the eating has finished, when the tables have been cleared. We take this to be art music, often in the form of a brief 'concert,' as distinguished from the functional music played while the guests were eating. In *The Decameron*, the group of young aristocrats which people this book are often described as participating in this type of music after the evening meal. On the evening before the stories of the first day, for example, we find,

> the tables being cleared away, the queen (the person in charge for the day) bade that instruments of music be brought, for all the ladies knew how to dance, as also the young men, and some of them could both play and sing excellently well. Accordingly, at her bidding, Dyoneo took a lute and Fiammetta a viol and began softly to sound a dance; whereupon the queen and the other ladies, together

---

28 *Amorous Fiammetta*, 182.

29 *Theseus*, XI, 63.

30 *L'Ameto*, 24ff.

31 Ibid., 31.

32 *Decameron*, I, 10.

with the two young men … struck up a round and began to dance with slow pace a roundelay; which ended, they fell to singing amorous and merry tunes. They continued thus till it seemed to the queen time to go to sleep.[33]

A similar description is found at the end of the first day.

Supper ended, the queen called for instruments of music and bade Lauretta leap up a dance, while Emilia sang a song, to the accompaniment of Dyoneo's lute.[34]

At the end of the second day, they again danced and sang, but also played instrumental works.[35]

Before the commencement of the stories of the third day, the group sang 'half a dozen canzonets' and danced *before* the meal, and again *after* the meal they 'gave themselves anew to music making and singing and dancing.'[36] At the end of the third day, again 'as soon as the tables were taken away,' Lauretta is asked to sing a song, for which Boccaccio again provides the lyrics and also an interesting aesthetic clue, 'in a somewhat plaintive style.'[37]

> No maid disconsolate
> Hath cause as I, alas!
> Who sigh for love in vain, to mourn her fate.

Some additional interesting aesthetic descriptions are found in the singing before the tales of the sixth day. Here we are told that the company sang 'goodly and pleasant' canzonets and then later four people sang 'in concert,' implying perhaps a four-part song.[38] Another clue to the style of these songs is found in the description of the singing after 'the food and tables were removed' before the tales of the seventh day. Here the company sang 'more blithely than ever.'[39]

Most of these references to art music clearly imply that people were carefully listening to the music, as opposed to hearing background music. Indeed, the presence of the contemplative listener is a central feature of art music. A particularly vivid portrait of such a listener is found in Boccaccio's pastoral romance, *L'Ameto*.

---

33 Ibid., I, 25ff.

34 Ibid., I, 74. Boccaccio provides here the lyrics for this song, a ballad, the first of a number of such lyrics he provides. On the evening before the eighth day, 'they ate with mirth and delight and afterwards sang.' [Ibid., II, 554] and at the end of the eighth day, they again sang after the meal [Ibid., II, 646]. At the end of the tenth day, the company, again after dinner, 'fell to singing and caroling and making music' [Ibid., II, 793].

35 Ibid., I, 193.

36 Ibid., I, 197. Performing music before the meal is described again at the beginning of the fifth day (Ibid., 367).

37 Ibid., I, 283. Afterward, 'diverse other songs were sung.'

38 Ibid., II, 445.

39 Ibid., II, 488.

> ... as if beside himself, he gazed fixedly at the singer. At this point her song ended, and after a long pause he gave a start—like one suddenly recalled to consciousness from a deep sleep.[40]

In this same work, a contemplative listener says he 'remained beside myself for a good time in a happiness never before known' and at the conclusion of the performance he begins by saying, 'when I returned to my senses.'[41] Yet another listener is captured by the music.

> Ameto lingered, listening to the song of the ladies, graced with a happy spirit ... and feeling surrendered his ears and his heart to sweet thoughts.[42]

Another description of the contemplative listener is found in *Theseus*, where a Venus hears 'delightful singing and every musical instrument' and is described as 'rapt out of herself.'[43] And surely the contemplative listener is implied in a comment describing the conclusion of a song sung by Dyoneo, at the end of the fifth day in *The Decameron*.

> Dyoneo, *by his silence*, showing that his song was ended ...[44]

There are a number of other specific references to contemplative listeners in *The Decameron*. At the conclusion of Elissa's song, at the end of the sixth day, we are told that the listeners 'all marveled at the words.' Elissa, herself, ended her song 'with a very plaintive sigh.'[45] Similarly, for the song sung at the conclusion of the eighth day, we are told the company listened with 'attentive solicitude.'[46] Likewise, in the sixth story of the tenth day, a canzonet is sung for a king, 'who beheld and listened to them with ravishment.'[47]

In a performance of a song, for which Boccaccio provides the words, in the seventh story of the tenth day, we find the listeners enchanted, still and attentive.

> These words Minuccio forthwith set to a soft and plaintive melody, such as the matter thereof required ... King Pedro being still at table, he was bidden by him to sing somewhat to his viol. Thereupon he fell to singing the aforesaid song so sweetly that all who were in the royal hall appeared enchanted, so still and attentive were they all to listen.[48]

---

[40] *L'Ameto*, 10.

[41] Ibid., 143.

[42] Ibid., 139.

[43] *Theseus*, VII, 53.

[44] *Decameron*, I, 444.

[45] Ibid., II, 486.

[46] Ibid., II, 647.

[47] Ibid., II, 732.

[48] Ibid., II, 739.

Finally, at the end of his *The Decameron* Boccaccio refers to the receptive listener,

> Again, such as they are, these stories, like everything else, can work both harm and profit, according to the disposition of the listener.[49]

In another place, Boccaccio reflects on the mysterious way in which both music and speech draw in the listener.

> Why do we neglect eloquence, by the cultivation of which we delight our ears and at the same time gratify our intellect? So certain moderate sounds of stringed instruments bring their delights into the minds. At first they seem with their sweetness to lead the mind into relaxation; then from all sides the sound finally collects everything into itself.
>
> In the same way well-polished speech flows into the mind by way of the ears, and it first soothes the mind by its brilliance. Then after it has driven away all other ideas, this skill so draws its audience to it that if you observe the audience, you will see that they are transfixed and unable to move, and that they all agree with the ideas of the speaker.[50]

By way of contrast, in one of his stories Boccaccio presents a musician who cannot find the necessary inspiration, resulting in listeners who are clearly not caught up in the experience.

> At the same time they lent their ears to Ameto's song; but it seemed to him as if the gods had not given him heed—for [the listeners] hindered him with pleasant quips, jeering now and then.[51]

The spirit of the troubadours was clearly still present in fourteenth-century Italy. In the case of Boccaccio, this presents a curious problem. On one hand he left poetry which has many of the characteristics of that style. But on the other hand, there are many passages in his works, especially among his later works, which treat women, generally, in a manner no troubadour would have understood. A typical example of the latter attitude is found in his book, *Concerning Famous Women*, where he observes, 'these things cannot be accomplished without a great deal of talent, which in women is usually very scarce.'[52] In this same book, in fact, he gives a rather clear description of his view of women's place, which includes avoiding singing!

> If a woman is to be considered completely chaste, it is necessary above all for her to curb her lustful and wandering eyes and confine them to the fringe of her dress. Her words must be not only respectable but brief, and she must speak only at the proper time. She must avoid idleness as a sure and deadly enemy of chastity, and she must abstain from feasting, for Venus is weak without food and wine. She must avoid singing and dancing as arrows of lasciviousness, and attend to temperance and sobriety. She must take care of her house, close her ears to shameful conversation, and avoid roaming from place to place. She must reject paint, superfluous perfumes, and ornaments. She must trample with all her strength on harmful thoughts and appetites, persist in sacred thoughts, and be vigilant.

---

49 Ibid., II, 796.

50 'Against the Detractors of Rhetoric,' in *The Fates of Illustrious Men*, 167ff.

51 *L'Ameto*, 42.

52 'Irene,' in *Concerning Famous Women*, 131.

And, not to discuss the entire subject of real chastity, she must love only her husband with great affection and scorn others, unless it is to love them with brotherly love. She must not go without shame in her face and breast to her husband's embrace, even when it is for the sake of procreation.[53]

It is no surprise, then, that in the introduction to the fourth day of his *The Decameron*, he pretends that the tradition of praising women, found in the troubadour repertoire of the thirteenth century, is now no longer in fashion. 'Others, making a show of wishing to speak more maturely,' he says, 'have said that it now ill sorts with my age to [write] of women or to [try] to please them.'[54] He writes that it is good to be inspired by the [women] gods, the 'Muses on Parnassus,' whereas contemporary women, while they look like the women gods, do not match them in worth. Nevertheless, he admits that contemporary women have inspired him to write poetry in the earlier style.

> If they pleased me for nought else, for this they would please me; because women have ere now been to me the occasion of composing a thousand verses, whereas the Muses never were to me the occasion of making any.[55]

In his works inspired by ancient literature, such as his romantic epic *Theseus*, women are more kindly characterized. When these women sing, we are inclined to think Boccaccio's description may reflect singing he had actually heard.

> Barefoot and clad in her shift, she entertained herself by singing amorous songs … Singing and taking her delight … she wove her garland with many flowers, all the while lightheartedly singing charming love lyrics with her angelic voice.[56]

Boccaccio mentions church music only in passing. One type is funeral music, as for example in his discussion of the plague in *The Decameron*, where Boccaccio mentions the 'funeral pomp of chants and candles.'[57] Funeral music is mentioned again in *Theseus*, where he also provides a few adjectives to describe the actual music.

> The kings arrived there and the mournful trumpet with its melancholy music was made ready …
> They ordered the trumpet played and the sad laments of the mourners … found their voice.[58]

---

53 'Sulpicia,' in Ibid., 147.
54 *Decameron*, I, 287.
55 Ibid., I, 291.
56 *Theseus*, III, 8 and 10.
57 *Decameron*, I, 13.
58 *Theseus*, X, 5.

Another passing reference to church music is found in the first story of the seventh day of *The Decameron*, where Boccaccio mentions the 'Laudsingers of Santa Maria Novella,' an order centered in Florence. They were particularly active during Lent, when their *laude* were even set to popular melodies. In this same story there is a reference to a hymn attributed to St. Ambrose, the 'Te lucis,' sung at the end of the day to protect one from evil dreams.[59]

The most revealing of these brief references to church music is found in the context of a discussion in the defense of Rhetoric. Again, it is only in passing that Boccaccio mentions,

> It is not becoming to reveal the spirit of our thoughts to the Creator of all things in a disorganized way, or to sing His praise in words that are not melodious.[60]

Boccaccio also makes a few passing references to the music of the theater. In his *Theseus*, Boccaccio mentions the audience of the theater 'awaiting the third blast of the Tyrrhenian sound,'[61] which is a reference to the medieval tradition of the playing of three trumpet fanfares to signal the beginning of the play. The extended fanfare in the seventeenth-century *Orfeo*, which Monteverdi specifies is to be repeated three times, is in recognition of this long tradition. In this same book, Boccaccio mentions a painting of a theater scene showing the 'joyful sound of the different musical instruments, and the likenesses of all of them.'[62]

We have mentioned above that music performed at banquets, when the eating was concluded and after the tables had been cleared, was usually art music. Boccaccio does, however, give us in one instance a description of music being performed while the guests were eating, thus entertainment music.

> The silver trays offered abundant food and the fine gold gave delicious wines to the thirsty; indeed the royal halls were soon to be seen filled with noble youths at every table; and the many and various musical sounds often caused the glittering hall to tremble.[63]

In another book, he mentions the entertainment music of banquets of a much lower order, 'we may … hear entertainers sing their dirty songs at banquets.'[64] Needless to say, our serious Boccaccio seems not to have enjoyed such scenes.

> Do you think those who spend their time at great banquets and drinking are happy? Far from it. They are weak and soft from their indolence.[65]

---

59 *Decameron*, II, 489, 491; see also, III, 881, 882.
60 'Against the Detractors of Rhetoric,' in *The Fates of Illustrious Men*, 166.
61 *Theseus*, VIII, 1.
62 Ibid., XI, 85.
63 *L'Ameto*, 103.
64 *Genealogia Deorum Gentilium*, XIV, xviii.
65 'Against Riches, the Frenzy of Many,' in *The Fates of Illustrious Men*, 109ff.

In *The Decameron*, at the end of the ninth day, we find *after dinner* music which appears to have been songs of an entertainment nature, described as,

> perhaps a thousand canzonets, more amusing in their words than masterful in their music.[66]

Boccaccio also describes elaborate entertainment music performed as part of the celebration of weddings.

> And after that the new Bride was come home, and the magnificent pomp used at the Tables was ended, and everyone with his passing dainty cakes and heavenly Nectar had cheered up their frolic minds, as divers brave dances, sometimes directed by the tuned voice of some cunning and singular Musician, and other some led and footed by the sound of divers sweet instruments, were begun, every place of the espousal house resounding with a general applause of mirth and joy.[67]

Due to his advanced age, our narrator could only in retrospect identify with such joyous celebration.

> And it grieved me no less to see myself deprived of the occasion of making such kind of joy, and enjoying such content, than I was sorrowful for the pleasure which I lost by [not hearing the] performance of the same. But from thence applying my ears to amorous delights, songs and sundry tunes, and remembering those with myself that were passed, I sighed, and marvelous desirous to see the end of such tedious feasts, being malcontent in the meantime, and sorrowful with myself, I passed them away.[68]

Another kind of entertainment music mentioned by Boccaccio was the 'noise of Trumpets, and of other martial instruments,' played during tournaments while the riders rode toward their targets.[69]

Finally, in the writings of Boccaccio there is an occasional reference to genuine popular folk music. He mentions common people singing 'ribald songs' in *The Decameron*,[70] and, in fact, actually gives us the title of one, 'Alas! who can the ill Christian be, that stole my pot away?'[71]

---

[66] *Decameron*, II, 698.

[67] *Amorous Fiammetta*, 169.

[68] Ibid., 168.

[69] Ibid., 196.

[70] *Decameron*, I, 18.

[71] Ibid., I, 331. The editor of this translation notes, without source, that three versions of this song are extant from this period.

Geoffrey Chaucer on Music

GEOFFREY CHAUCER (1340–1400) was the first great figure of English literature and certainly her greatest writer of the fourteenth century. The man saw much of life, fighting in France in 1357 and making diplomatic journeys to Italy in 1372 and 1378. As a result, he gives us a broad view of fourteenth-century English life, including the role of music. Indeed, one is struck by the constant presence of music throughout all levels of society. Among the ordinary people of his famous *Canterbury Tales*,[1] which describes a group of people meeting in a tavern on their pilgrimage to the shrine of Becket at Canterbury, the Knight, Squire, Prioress, Friar, Miller, a Cook's apprentice, Pardoner, Sumner, a carpenter's wife, Nicholas the poor scholar and Absalom the parish clerk were all performing musicians. The Squire, in particular, attracts our attention. Described as a lover and soldier, but without reference to being educated, he stands as a symbol of the importance of music as part of being a cultured person in the Renaissance. We would not have found one such as him before the fourteenth century. How many young men today could equal his accomplishments? Leaving aside the fact that he could ride a horse well, dance and draw, he is described as singing or playing the flute all day and could compose and notate his own music!

> Syngynge he was or floytynge al the day
> He was a fressh as is the monthe of May.
> Short was his gowne, with sleves longe and wyde.
> Wel koude he sitte on hors and faire ryde.
> He koude songes make and wel endite [notate],
> Juste and eek daunce, and weel purtreye and write.[2]

The reader should note that when Chaucer intends art, as we use the term, he uses the word 'craft.' When he uses the word art, as a noun, he usually means the 'liberal arts.' In such references to scholars of the liberal arts, Chaucer nearly always adds that they are poorly paid—as they are today! In 'The Miller's Tale,' for example, we read of 'a poor scholar, who had studied the liberal arts.'

> With hym ther was dwellynge a poure scoler,
> Hadde lerned art …[3]

---

[1] Unless otherwise indicated, the line designations correspond to the version of the *Canterbury Tales, The Complete Works of Geoffrey Chaucer* (Boston: Houghton Mifflin, 1933).

[2] 'Prologue, The Canterbury Tales,' 91ff.

[3] 'The Miller's Tale,' 3189.

And in another place he mentions the poor scholar's threadbare cape,

> With a thredbare cope, as is a povre scoler …[4]

The philosophers, being another type of scholar, were also ones with little money.

> But al be that he was a philosophre,
> Yet hadde he but litel gold in cofre …[5]

Perhaps this contributed to Chaucer's observation in 'The Reeve's Tale,' that he 'cares not a weed' for philosophers and their art!

> Of al hir art I counte noght a tare.[6]

One of the hallmarks of the early Renaissance humanists was a renewed interest in the writings of the ancient Greek philosophers and among these writings they rediscovered the concept of the 'music of the spheres.' Chaucer was also interested in this idea and the music of the nine spheres, he contends, is the original source for melody and harmony in the world.

> And after shewede he hym the nyne speres,
> And after that the melodye herde he
> That cometh of thilke speres thryes thre,
> That welle is of musik and melodye
> In this world here, and cause of armonye.[7]

It is interesting that Chaucer distinguishes between Reason and the emotions, almost as if he were aware of the existence of the right and left hemispheres of the brain. In 'The Romaunt of the Rose,' for example, a lover, after becoming lost in the feelings of love, rediscovers his rational self.

> And hadde witt, and my felyng.[8]

In an even more interesting passage, Chaucer seems to suggest that a character should use both halves of the brain, as it were, to fully comprehend.

> You must both perceive *and* feel that pride is a sin.[9]

---

[4] Prologue, 'The Canterbury Tales,' 260.
[5] Ibid., 297.
[6] 'The Reeve's Tale,' 4056.
[7] 'The Parliament of the Birds,' 59ff.
[8] 'The Romaunt of the Rose,' 1738.
[9] Ibid., 2240.

Chaucer, following centuries of Church writers, also suggests that it is Reason which must keep the emotions under control. In 'The Merchant's Tale,' the advice is given that, in order not to hinder one's salvation, the lust of one's wife must be controlled by skill and reason. Not pleasing her *too* amorously keeps one from other sins.

> In mariage, ne nevere mo shal bee,
> That yow shal lette of youre savacion,
> So that ye use, as skile is and reson,
> The lustes of youre wyf attemprely,
> And that ye plese hire nat to amorously,
> And that ye kepe yow eek from oother synne.[10]

This was possible because Chaucer understood both Reason and the emotions to be housed in the mind.

> Have pacience and resoun in youre mynde![11]
> ……
> And moche sorwe hadde he in his mynde …[12]

That being the case, it seemed to him to follow naturally that Reason could control emotion, for as he said in one case, 'If you don't think of pain, you will feel none!'[13] But this is not to say that Reason can *explain* the emotions. Especially in the example of a man falling in love, Chaucer wonders, 'Who can find Reason or wit in this?'

> That men shulde loven alwey causeles,
> Who can a resound fynde or wit in that?[14]

On the whole, one gets the impression that Chaucer himself valued what he had learned by experience more than what he had gained by conceptual information, such as we would associate with Reason. Even when he mentions 'science,' it is usually a reference to some practical knowledge, rather than formal or speculative knowledge. It follows that Chaucer says we should trust books only in the absence of personal experience. 'We should honor and believe these old books, where there is no test other than experience.'[15] Indeed, in numerous places Chaucer clearly states that various kinds of knowledge is proven only by experience. For example, with regard to the fact that there is a limit to one's lifespan, Chaucer says we need

---

[10] 'The Merchant's Tale,' 1676.
[11] 'The Romaunt of the Rose,' 2369.
[12] 'The Legend of Good Women,' III, 946.
[13] 'Troilus and Criseyde,' IV, 466.
[14] 'The Parliament of the Birds,' 590.
[15] 'The Legend of Good Women,' 27.

no authority for this, as it is proven by experience.[16] Or regarding the significance of dreams, 'This has been well founded by experience.'[17] Even, Chaucer says, where the Bible does not suffice, experience will teach you.

> And yf that hooly writ may nat suffyse,
> Experience shal the teche.[18]

However much Chaucer valued experience, he also recognized, in an almost Darwinian sense, that we are in some way programmed by Nature. In 'The Squire's Tale,' for example,

> That Nature in youre principles hath set.[19]

It follows, as well, that one can act against these principles.

> It is agayns the proces of nature.[20]

Chaucer attributes this kind of understanding to a frequently mentioned goddess of Nature,[21] whom, in turn, is the 'vicaire of the almyghty Lord.'[22]

Chaucer's references to the emotions suggest that he viewed them as natural and common to every man, as when he says 'Every happy man has a full delicate feeling.'[23] Emotions are real, and can be expressed through speech, as in 'A Complaint to his Lady,' where a character says, 'For truly I *say*, as I *feel*.'[24] He also gives an example of non-verbal expression of emotions, when Troilus gives a gentle sigh as an expression of his internal emotions,

> That shewed his affeccioun withinne.[25]

---

[16] 'The Knight's Tale,' 3001.

[17] 'The Nun's Priest's Tale,' 4168.

[18] 'L'Envoy de Chaucer a Bukton,' 21. For additional references to understanding being proven by experience, see 'The Wife of Bath's Tale,' 468; 'The Friar's Tale,' 1517; 'The Sumner's Tale,' 2057; 'The Merchant's Tale,' 2238; 'Troilus and Criseyde,' III, 1283; 'The House of Fame,' II, 370; and 'Romaunt of the Rose,' 5553.

[19] 'The Squire's Tale,' 487. See also 'The House of Fame,' I, 490 and III, 276; 'The Legend of Good Women,' 975; and 'The Complaint of Venus,' 14.

[20] 'The Franklin's Tale,' 1345. See also 'The Romaunt of the Rose, ' 4769.

[21] For references to the goddess of Nature, see the first 'Parson's Tale,' 450–460; 'The Book of the Duchess,' 870; 'The Parliament of Birds,' 303, 368, 639; and 'The Romaunt of the Rose,' 4871.

[22] 'The Parliament of Birds,' 379.

[23] 'Boece,' IV, 108.

[24] 'A Complaint to his Lady,' 55.

[25] 'Troilus and Criseyde,' III, 1364.

It is interesting that twice in 'The Legend of Good Women,' Chaucer raises the question whether emotions can be pretended. First he says, yes, it is possible to 'counterfeit pain and woe.'[26] Later, however, in 'The Legend of Phillis,' a character doubts that anyone has the ability to fake 'such tears.'

> 'How coude ye wepe so by craft' quod she,
> 'May there swiche teres feyned be?'[27]

For Chaucer, love was the most strongly felt emotion, an emotion so strong that one can entirely lose one's sense of self. In 'Troilus and Criseyde,' Criseyde kisses Troilus until he was 'so full of joy he knew not where his spirit was.'

> That where his spirit was, for joie he nyste.[28]

Chaucer usually presents pleasure and pain as opposites, as in 'For joy is contrarie unto sorowe.'[29] In one place he associates joy with heaven, which he opposes with pain and hell.

> A thousand tymes have I herd men telle
> That ther ys joy in hevene and peyne in helle,
> And I accorde wel that it ys so.[30]

On the other hand, he adds his contribution to a thought frequently found in ancient literature, that Love consists of *both* pleasure and pain.

> A peyne also it is joious.[31]

This admixture of pleasure and pain in love sometimes leaves the lover suffering a confusion of his feelings, weeping in laughter and singing while lamenting.

> Wepinge to laughe, and singe in compleynyng ...[32]

One poor lover is so confused he declares, 'joy or sorrow, whatsoever it be—I have no feelings [at all].'

> Joye or sorowe, wherso hyt be—
> For I have felynge in nothyng ...[33]

---

26 'The Legend of Good Women,' 1376.
27 Ibid., 2528.
28 'Troilus and Criseyde,' III, 1351.
29 'The Romaunt of the Rose,' 348.
30 'The Legend of Good Women,' 1ff.
31 'The Romaunt of the Rose,' 4733, and again in 5252.
32 'The Complaint of Venus,' 28.
33 'The Book of the Duchess,' 10.

Chaucer adds that bachelors, not having love, often experience only pain and woe.[34]

Finally, in his references to pleasure and pain, Chaucer several times uses music as a synonym for joy or pleasure, as if the comparison were not 'Pleasure and Pain,' but 'Music and Pain.' Thus, Troilus asks, 'Shall I now weep or sing?'[35] Similarly, a girl in 'The Man of Law's Tale' is told she must depart, whether 'she wepe or synge.'[36]

One cannot expect to find, by the fourteenth century, much definition of the aesthetics of art as we think of it today. Except for music, art was still what it was since the world of ancient Greece, something thought of as a craft. Nevertheless, in Chaucer we begin to see, characteristics which clearly extend beyond 'craft.' First of all, in 'The House of Fame,' he makes it clear that beauty is something which words cannot describe.

> So that the grete craft, beaute,
> The cast, the curiosite
> Ne kan I not to yow devyse;
> My wit ne may me not suffise.[37]

All the best poetic expressions of beauty having been taken by earlier poets, Chaucer protests, 'Others have garnered the corn and I, coming after, am lucky to find an ear.' And once again, a character, upon seeing the face of a lady, declares that he lacks both the language and the wit to describe such beauty.

> But which a visage had she thertoo!
> Allas! myn herte ys wonder woo
> That I ne kan discryven hyt!
> Me lakketh both Englyssh and wit
> For to undo hyt at the fulle;
> And eke my spirites be so dulle
> So gret a thyng for to devyse.[38]

We also note that he recognized the element of inspiration as something needed for attaining a success beyond that of mere workmanship. In his 'Troilus and Criseyde,' based on Boccaccio's, *Filostrato*, Chaucer begs the Muse, Cleo, to inspire him to succeed in rhyming this poem in English, which he is taking from the Latin. 'I need here none other art but thine.'

> O lady myn, that called art Cleo,
> Thow be my speed fro this forth, and my Muse,
> To ryme wel this book til I have do;
> Me nedeth here noon other art to use.[39]

---

34 'The Merchant's Tale,' 1278.
35 'Troilus and Criseyde,' II, 952.
36 'The Man of Law's Tale,' 294.
37 'The House of Fame,' III, 1177.
38 'The Book of the Duchess,' 895ff.
39 'Troilus and Criseyde,' II, 7ff.

Aside from pointing out that beauty is something which cannot be described in words, the most specific definition which Chaucer offers for beauty is that it is *Truth*. 'Truth,' he says, 'is the crown of Beauty'[40] This relationship between beauty and Truth is, we believe, closely related in Chaucer's thinking on the ancient association between art and nature, for he also points out 'Nature does not lie.'[41]

On the other hand, Chaucer pays tribute to the thought of the ancient Greeks, that art imitates nature, however he generally implies that this cannot be perfectly done—hence, for example, his choice of a word to mean 'imitates.'

> As craft countrefeteth kynde.[42]

Indeed, in 'The Physician's Tale,' Nature herself addresses this point. 'I,' says Nature, 'can form and color a creature—who can imitate me?' Not Pygmalion, not Apelles or Zeuxis, for 'the Principal Former [God] has made me his vicar-general to form and paint earthly creatures as I will.'

> Lo! I, Nature,
> Thus kan I forme and peynte a creature,
> Whan that me list; who kan me countrefete?[43]

Finally, after the rediscovery of the ancient Greek Tragedies, there was some speculation among the humanists as to the role of music in these plays—some even contending that the entire plays were sung. Chaucer also refers to the importance of music in the original productions of Greek Tragedy, when he says Tragedy is nothing other than crying and bewailing *in song*, Fortune's attacks upon proud thrones.

> Traagedi's noon oother maner thyng
> Ne kan in syngyng crie ne biwaille
> But that Fortune alwey wole assaille
> With unwar strook the regnes that been proude.[44]

Chaucer makes the aesthetic point that music is not just sounds made on musical instruments, but rather music is something beyond those sounds. He does this in 'Troilus and Criseyde,' where Pandarus observes that an ass hears the sound of a man playing the harp, but it, being a beast, does not hear the *music*, 'no melody can sink in to his mind to gladden him.'

> Or artow lik an asse to the harpe,
> That hereth sown whan men the strynges plye,

---

[40] 'A Complaint unto Pity,' 75.
[41] 'The Parliament of Birds,' 629.
[42] 'The House of Fame,' III, 1212.
[43] 'The Physician's Tale,' 11ff.
[44] 'The Monk's Tale,' 3951.

> But in his mynde of that no melodie
> May sinken hym to gladen, for that he
> So dul ys of his bestialite.[45]

Regarding the purpose of music, we find a very interesting comment in 'The Book of the Duchess,'[46] especially in view of the medieval division between *speculative* music (conceptual) and *practical* music (performance). When a character is speaking of whether Jubal invented music, as related in the Old Testament, or Pythagoras, another character responds that none of that matters and as for himself, 'I put my feeling into songs, to gladden my heart.' Chaucer touches here upon the very essence of music—expression of feelings. The use of music to 'gladden,' is, of course, one of the most frequently given purposes of music in all ancient and medieval literature.

Another reference to the importance of *feeling* in music is found in the 'Nun's Priest's Tale,' where a fox who has come to hear a rooster sing, declares that the rooster sings with more feeling in his music than Boethius or any singer.

> Therwith ye han in musyk moore feelynge
> Than hadde Boece, or any that kan synge.[47]

Later in this same passage, Chaucer observes that the best singer is one who sings from the heart.[48]

In this regard, since the importance of the expression of feeling and emotions in music is associated in more modern times with the fact that music can express what words cannot, it is interesting that the miller, in 'The Miller's Tale,' could play on his gittern and sing in a loud voice, yet was 'bashful of speech.'[49]

Another interesting reference to music as an expression of feeling is found in 'The Romaunt of the Rose,' where a musician's feelings toward unfaithful women is expressed by *discordant* music.[50]

Returning to the purpose of music, earlier in the passage cited above from 'The Book of the Duchess,' another purpose for music is given as, 'to keep me from idleness.' Here the speaker makes the interesting observation that he had made many songs, but could 'not make them so well, nor knew all the art,' which, of course, carries the suggestion that there was a recognized 'art' to this form of composition.

> Althogh I koude not make so wel
> Songes, ne knewe the art al.[51]

---

45 'Troilus and Criseyde,' I, 731ff.
46 'The Book of the Duchess,' 1172.
47 'Nun's Priest's Tale,' 4483
48 Ibid., 4491.
49 'The Miller's Tale,' 3333.
50 'The Romaunt of the Rose,' 4247ff.
51 'The Miller'sTale,' 1160.

Another frequently given purpose for music in both ancient and medieval literature is for the purpose of solace. Thus in 'The Romaunt of the Rose,' a singer specifically sings to 'solace the folk,'

> To syngen first, folk to solace.[52]

In 'Troilus and Criseyde,' Troilus begins a song which also has the purpose of overcoming sorrow.[53]

On the other hand, sometimes sadness is so great that even music can not 'gladden the heart.' When Criseyde was away, Troilus was so sad that he could not bear to hear (instrumental) music and thought no one should make music.

> Syn that he saugh his lade was aweye,
> It was his sorwe upon him for to sen,
> Or for to here on instruments so pleye.
> For she, that of his herte berthe the keye,
> Was absent, lo, this was his fantasie,
> That no wight sholde maken melodie.[54]

A similar thought is expressed in a poem known as 'A.B.C.,' in which a plea is addressed to the Virgin Mary for solace, as 'no music or song can aid us in our adversity.'

> We han noon oother melodye or glee
> Us to rejoyse in oure adversitee.[55]

Additional examples can be found in 'The Knight's Tale,' where even music cannot cheer up a sad lover,[56] and in 'The Book of the Duchess,' when a character tells us that not even Orpheus, the god of music, can make his sorrow pass.[57] The same god of music, Orpheus, appears under his alternate name, Phoebes, in 'The Manciple's Tale,' where in his sadness he actually destroys his musical instruments!

> For sorwe of which he brak his mynstralcie,
> Bothe harpe, and lute, and gyterne, and sautrie ...[58]

---

52 'The Romaunt of the Rose,' 756.
53 'Troilus and Criseyde,' I, 389.
54 Ibid., V, 456.
55 'A.B.C.,' 100.
56 'The Knight's Tale,' 1367.
57 'The Book of the Duchess,' 569.
58 'The Manciple's Tale,' 267.

Given this broad view of the purposes of music, one can appreciate the fact that Chaucer also believed variety was an important value in performance. In one place he observes that even the best harpist alive, with the best sounding harp and the most pointed plectrum, would never play on just one string or play just one song, for everyone's 'ears would grow dull.'[59]

As was the case with the ancient Greeks, the adjective 'sweet' is found in Chaucer as a synonym for the most beautiful music. In 'The Parliament of Birds,' we read of string instruments playing music of 'ravishing sweetness.'

> Of instruments of strenges in accord
> Herde I so pleye a ravyshyng swetnesse.[60]

In this same passage, however, birds are given an even higher compliment, for their music is the voice of angels.

> On every bow the bryddes herde I synge,
> With voys of aungel in here armonye.

In 'The Books of the Duchess,' Chaucer again speaks of birds singing, some low and some high, with 'sweetness,' in tune, with 'so merry a harmony, so sweet strains' and observes 'nowhere was ever heard instrument or melody yet half so sweet or of half so well in accord.' When he also mentions that none merely pretended to sing, but all did not spare their voices, not to mention the reference to 'the most solemn service,' we are inclined to wonder if this passage were intended not as a description of birds, but a metaphor for the best choral singing Chaucer had heard.

> With smale foules a gret hep
> That had affrayed me out of my slep,
> Thorgh noyse and swetness of her song.
> And, as me mette, they sate among
> Upon my chambre roof wythoute,
> Upon the tyles, overal aboute,
> And songen, everch in hys wyse,
> The moste solemne servise
> By noote, that ever man, y trowe,
> Had herd; for some of hem song lowe,
> Som high, and al of oon acord.
> To telle shortly, att oo word.
> Was never herd so swete a steven,—
> But hyt had be a thyng of heven,—
> So mery a soun, so swete entewnes,
> That certes, for the toun of Tewnes,
> I nolde but I had herd hem synge;

---

[59] Ibid., II, 1030.

[60] 'The Parliament of Birds,' 197.

> For al my chambre gan to rynge
> Thurgh syngynge of her armonye.
> For instrument nor melodye
> Was nowhere herd yet half so swete,
> Nor of acorde half so mete;
> For ther was noon of hem that feyned
> To synge, for ech of hem hym peyned
> To fynde out mery crafty notes.
> They ne spared not her throtes.[61]

Finally, we treat separately the remarkable poem, 'The House of Fame,' for it offers some of Chaucer's most extensive descriptions of fourteenth-century musical practice.

THE HOUSE OF FAME

The general musician of the thirteenth century, the *jongleur*, gives way in the fourteenth century to the more specialized *minstrel*, who is usually a wind player.[62] The jongleur remains the lesser, wandering musician, whom Chaucer in one place equates with the Golliard, the unemployed, wandering students and clergy of the thirteenth century.[63] The general disfavor in which these wandering musicians were now held can be seen in Chaucer's declaration that 'a jongleur is abominable to God!'[64]

During the fourteenth century, the institutions called minstrel schools, *scolae ministrallorum*, appear and can be documented in considerable instances. During Lent, when performances were not allowed, the more respected minstrels from throughout Europe would gather each year in a town willing to be host, usually in the Low Countries, in great numbers—one Italian town in 1324 is said to have hosted 1,500 minstrels.[65] It was in these gatherings, 'schools,' that the minstrels traded instruments and especially learned new, international repertoire, '*pour apprendre des nouvelles chansons.*'[66]

Other than a number of references of various nobles sending their minstrels to these schools, and documentation of the various towns which hosted them, there is no literature which describes them—these were players, not writers. It is with this perspective, then, that our attention is drawn to a passage in Book III of Chaucer's *House of Fame*.[67] We believe this passage, which has been overlooked by musicologists, is a rare description by someone who had actually observed one of these minstrel schools. While this poem takes the form of a dream, we suspect that he could *only* have imagined such a description of a large gathering

---

[61] 'The Book of the Duchess,' 295ff.

[62] String players are sometimes called, 'string minstrels,' and singers 'mouth minstrels' (*menetriers de bouche*).

[63] 'Prologue, The Canterbury Tales,' 560.

[64] 'The Manciple's Tale,' 343.

[65] Romain Goldron, Minstrels and Masters (H.S. Stuttman), 38.

[66] Walter Salmen, Der Fahrende Musiker im Europaischen Mittelalter (Kassel, 1960), 181ff.

[67] 'House of Fame,' 1197ff.

of wind instrument minstrels if he had at some point witnessed one of these 'schools.' And it is the extraordinarily large number of instrumentalists in particular which first attracts our attention. Of the wind instrument players, he says he saw 'many thousand times twelve!' There were others, playing instruments whose names he did not know, and they were more numerous 'than there be stars in heaven.' These he says he won't bother to name because it would take too much time and 'time lost can in no way be recovered.' He concludes his description of players with the lowly jongleurs, some of whom were also famous and whose name he knew. But, again, to list them all, he says, 'would take from now until doomsday!'

The possibility that this description was inspired by his having observed a minstrel school is strengthened by his reference to the presence of famous players, as well as foreign visitors ('Pipers of the Duche tonge') and his specific mention that they all came 'to lerne.' It may be our only first-hand description of one of these schools.

> Ful the castel alle aboute,
> Of alle maner of mynstralles
> And gestiours that tellen tales
> ......
>
> Tho saugh I stonden hem behynde,
> Afer fro hem, al be hemselve,
> Many thousand tymes twelve,
> That maden lowde mynstralcyes
> In cornemuse and shalemyes,
> And many other maner pipe,
> That craftely begunne to pipe
> Bothe in doucet and in rede,
> That ben at festes with the brede,
> And many flowte and liltyng-horne,
> And pipes made of grfene corne
> ......
>
> Ther saugh I famous, olde and yonge,
> Pipers of the Duche tonge,
> To lerne love-daunces, sprynges,
> Reyes, and these strange thynges.
> ......
>
> There saugh I sitte in other se's,
> Pleyinge upon sondry gle's,
> Whiche that I kan not nevene,
> Moo than sterres ben in hevene,
> Of whiche I nyl as now not ryme,
> For ese of yow, and los of tyme.
> For tyme ylost, this knowen ye,
> Be no way may recovered be.
> There saugh I pleye jugelours,
> ......

> What shuld I make lenger tale
> Of alle the pepil y ther say,
> Fro hennes into domes day!

Following this passage, Chaucer then begins a long section which addresses the entitlement of various members of society to 'Fame,' for lasting reputation. Since music and several kinds of musicians also figure in this section we should also consider them as well, for their possible insights into his views on the aesthetics of music.

The narrator begins walking up a hill covered with the tombstones of 'famous folk,' but in every case the inscriptions had been worn by time and the names could no longer be read. The narrator observed that these names have been 'melted away by heat, and not worn away by storms.' He does not identify these people, but we cannot help but wonder if they were troubadours, those who melted away by heat [love], as compared to the wandering jongleurs who were out in the 'storms.'[68]

At the top of the hill are more tombstones, but on these the names can still be read, as they were protected against the elements by the castle. Do these represent those most fortunate of all minstrels, those hired, and thus protected, by nobles?

In another location, apart from the rest, is a space reserved for famous trumpeters, including some named in ancient literature and the Old Testament. These he associates with war, for in bloodsheding one gladly uses trumpet playing.

> Of hem that maken blody soun
> In trumpe, beme, and claryoun;
> For in fight and blod-shedynge
> Ys used gladly clarionynge.

Now he comes across a group of the lowest class of musicians, the true wandering beggar musicians. They are crying for hand-outs, yet the narrator mentions how ironic it is to see them clad in royal coats, with coat-of-arms from all over the world (castoff clothing being a common gift to such musicians). The whole class of thirteenth-century jongleurs and troubadours had often been criticized for being available to sing praise of a nobleman, for a fee, so here Chaucer also mentions those 'That crien ryche folkes laudes.'

Now, in this allegorical dream, we come upon the goddess of Fame herself who sits in judgment of various groups of people making their pleas for lasting fame.[69] To help dispense her judgments, she calls upon Aeolus, the god of the winds, to bring his trumpets [*clarioun*]. One of these is a trumpet of gold, called 'Clear Praise' [*Clere Laude*], and the other is black, made

---

[68] As in the *De Saint Pierre de du jongleor*:

> But quite often in his shirt
> Was exposed to wind and blast …

[69] Among these are poets and historians and one, whom is mentioned by name, the 'Englyssh Gaufride,' is thought by some scholars to be Chaucer himself.

of brass by the devil, and is called 'Slander.' When this black trumpet is blown, the sound, coming out as fast as a ball from a gun, is described as a foul noise, a kind of black, blue, red, greenish smoke, such as comes from the chimney where men melt lead.

> What dide this Eolus, but he
> Tok out hys blake trumpe of bras,
> That fouler than the devel was,
> and gan this trumpe for to blowe,
> As al the world shulde overthrowe,
> That thrughout every regioun
> Wente this foule trumpes soun,
> As swifte as pelet out of gonne,
> Whan fyr is in the poudre ronne.
> And such a smoke gan out wende
> Out of his foule trumpes ende,
> Blak, bloo, grenyssh, swartish red,
> As doth were that men melte led.

For a group of people who have done good works, but never received credit, the golden trumpet is blown. Presumably the golden trumpet was also blown for the next group, those who don't want credit, their good works having been done for goodness and for no other reason. 'I grant your wish,' says the goddess of Fame, 'let your works die!'

The following group also wanted no fame, for their works were done for God. 'What! are you mad?,' the goddess responds, 'You think you will do good and have no glory for it?' She has the golden trumpet 'ring out in music' their deeds for all the world to hear.

The next group is surely troubadours, for their 'good works' have all been done for women, for which 'women loved us madly,' but often rewarded only with brooches or rings. For all this hard work, they felt they deserved renown and the goddess agreed and had the golden trumpet play again.

Another group, though they were 'gluttonous swine and idle wretches full of the rotten vice of sloth,' thought they deserved fame on the same basis as the previous group, but the goddess had them condemned by the black trumpet. The following group of 'treacherous' people also received this reward.

In concluding this dream, the narrator provides the theme, 'I knew ever that folk have desired fame and glory and renown diversely. But truly till now I knew not how or where Fame dwelt; nor yet what manner of weight she is, in look or quality, nor the manner of her judgments, till the time I came hither.'

Finally, in this same poem, Chaucer makes several observations on the acoustics of music and sound.[70] Sound, he says, is nothing but broken air, thus all speech is nothing but air. Similarly, when a player strikes the harp strings, whether hard or lightly, 'the air breaks apart with the stroke.' When a pipe is blown 'sharp' [strongly], what we hear is the air 'twisted and rent with violence.' And, lastly, all sound tends to rise.

In his poetry Chaucer also includes references to true art music. He refers to songs or singing a great number of times in his poetry and many of these references remind one of the Troubadour, Trouvière and Minnesinger traditions of the previous century. In particular, we think of the character in 'The Legend of Good Women'[71] who composes songs for the lady, sends her letters, tokens brooches and rings and attends to her at dances and banquets, or the one who composed songs 'for the worship of Love' found in 'The House of Fame.'[72] In 'The Clerk of Oxford's Tale,' the clerk declares 'with heart fresh and lusty I will sing you a song to gladden you,'[73] which is all the more interesting to us for Chaucer provides the lyrics for this love song. In 'Troilus and Criseyde,' we find the lyrics for another love song.[74]

The troubadours also often sang welcome songs for the return of spring and summer, and Chaucer gives us the lyrics for such a song, although here sung by birds. Interestingly enough, he mentions that the melody of this song came from France.[75]

> Now welcome, somer, with thy sonne softe,
> That hast this wintres wedres overshake,
> And driven away the longe nyghtes blake!

In the allegorical story of the goddess of Fame, the description of accompanied songs which made the palace walls ring, is also quite similar to many such scenes in the troubadour poetry.

> And, Lord! the hevenyssh melodye
> Of songes, ful of armonye,
> I herde aboute her trone ysonge
> That al the paleys-walles ronge![76]

---

[70] 'The House of Fame,' II, 765ff.
[71] 'The Legend of Good Women,' 1268ff.
[72] 'The House of Fame,' 622ff.
[73] 'The Clerk's Tale,' 1173ff.
[74] 'Troilus and Criseyde,' I, 400ff.
[75] 'The Parliament of Birds,' 675ff.
[76] 'The House of Fame,' III, 1395.

An even more ancient tradition is the epic song, in which the singer sings of the deeds of heroes of the past. We find him in the tale of 'Sir Thopas,' where a minstrel is called for to sing tales of royalty, popes and cardinals.[77] In this same tradition are nineteen ladies who sing and dance a ballade, in 'carol style,'[78] the lyrics of which include reference to music in the Old Testament, Greece, Rome and Cleopatra.

A characteristic of the solo song which we do not find in the thirteenth century is 'loud' singing, which we take to mean enthusiasm. In the 'Canterbury Tales,' the carpenter's wife sang 'loud and lively'[79] and we are told that even a trumpet was not half so loud as the two-part songs sung by the Pardoner and the Sumner.[80] The parish clerk, Absalom, sometimes sang in a 'loud treble,'[81] but when he was thinking of love he sang in a small and gentle voice with good harmony from his gittern.

> He syngeth in his voys gentil and smal,
> 'Now, deere laady, if thy wille be,
> I praye yow that ye wole rewe on me,'
> Ful wel acordaunt to his gyternynge.[82]

We begin to find in the fourteenth century hints of performance which begin to have characteristics of 'concert' music. The Prior, when singing, appears to have enjoyed his listeners as much as they enjoyed his music, for 'his eyes twinkled in his head as the stars on a frosty night.'[83] Certainly we have a little concert by the wind minstrels[84] when we are told 'it was like heaven to listen to them.'

> Toforn hym gooth the loude mynstralcye,
> Til he cam to his chambre of parementz,
> Ther as they sownen diverse instrumentz,
> That it is lyk an heavene for to heere.[85]

Another place where one finds something similar to 'concert' music as we know it, is *after* the meal. Music played when the food is brought out, or when the people are eating, must be considered functional music. But often brief 'concerts' followed a meal and the key is if the

---

77 'Sir Thopas,' 845ff.

78 'The Legend of Good Women,' 200ff.

79 'The Miller's Tale,' 3257.

80 'Prologue, The Canterbury Tales,' 669.

81 'The Miller'sTale,' 3332.

82 Ibid., 3360. This musical parish clerk, could also serve as a barber, surgeon, lawyer and dance twenty different ways in the 'Oxford manner.'

83 'Prologue, The Canterbury Tales,' 266.

84 A frequent English synonym for the wind ensemble was 'loud minstrels.'

85 'The Squire's Tale,' 268ff.

guests are *listening* to the music. We find such a description in 'The Squire's Tale,' where after the third course, the king 'sat … listening to his minstrels play their things deliciously before him at the table.'

> Whil that this kyng sit thus in his nobleye,
> Herknynge his mynstralles hir thynges pleye
> Biforn hym at the bord deliciously.[86]

A singer we find especially attractive is Nicholas, the 'poor scholar' of Oxford. He sang only at night, in his room, for himself, sweetly singing to the accompaniment of his psaltery. But he sang a varied repertoire, some sacred songs and some secular ones, such as 'The King's Note.'

> And al above ther lay a gay sautrie,
> On which he made a-nyghtes melodie
> So swetely that all the cyhambre rong;
> And *Angelus ad virginem* he song;
> And after that he song the kynges noote.[87]

We find only one mention of true educational music in Chaucer, but it is a rather interesting one. It is a reference to the use of music to teach the Latin prayers of the Church.[88] A child in the church school hears the older students singing the *Alma redemptoris* daily. After repeatedly hearing this, the child himself soon knows the music and the first verse by heart, but, of course, he has no idea what it means. When he asks an older child, one of the singers, what the words mean, the older child says he has heard that it is a salute to 'our blessed Lady and pray her to be our help and succor when we die.' But, he brings into question the effectiveness of this kind of rote teaching by observing that he really can't say more about it, for 'I learn singing, but know little grammar.'

> I kan namoore expounde in this mateere;
> I lerne song, I kan but smal grammeere.

Chaucer also provides descriptions for the full range of fourteenth-century functional music. References to church music include the singing of the friars,

> Til that the belle of laudes gan to rynge,
> And freres in the chauncel gonne synge.[89]

---

[86] Ibid., 78.

[87] 'The Miller's Tale,' 3213.

[88] 'The Prioress's Tale,' 516ff.

[89] 'The Miller's Tale,' 3655.

and the prioress, Madame Eglantine, who sang the divine service 'intoned full seemly in her nose.'[90]

Chaucer describes in several places the music performed for marriage celebrations. First, we see the bachelor arriving with minstrels hired for the occasion.

> And of his retenue the bachelrye,
> With many a sound of sondry melodye,
> Unto the village of the which I tolde,
> In this array the righte wey han holde.[91]
> During one marriage ceremony the music is described as,
> And thus with alle blisse and melodye
> Hath Palamon ywedded Emelye.[92]

In another place the following wedding celebration included flowers, torches and 'the place full of the sound of minstrelsy, of the amorous songs of marriage.'[93]

In 'The Man of Law's Tale,' Chaucer seems to tire of such description. 'Why,' he asks, 'should I speak of the royal array at the marriage, what course went first at the banquet, who blows a horn or trumpet? Only the cream of every tale is to be set forth; there was eating and drinking, and folk danced and sang and made merry.'[94]

In 'The Knight's Tale' we find a description of an entire day on which a tournament is held. Since the tournament was, among other things, a form of practice for battle, it was usually the musical instruments used in battle which accompanied the tournament as well. In this case, the tournament is announced at the beginning of the day by,

> Pypes, trompes, nakers, clariounes,
> That in the bataille blowen blody sounes ...[95]

Next, these instruments lead the participants through the city in a procession to the lists where the tournament would be held.

> Up goon the trompes and the melodye,
> And to the lystes rit the compaignye,
> By ordinance, thurghout the citee large.[96]

Now, as the trumpets announce the start, there is no more to say—we will see, he says, who can joust and who can ride.

---

[90] 'Prologue, The Canterbury Tales,' 122.

[91] 'The Clerk's Tale,' 270ff.

[92] 'The Knight's Tale,' 3097.

[93] 'The Legend of Good Women,' 2615.

[94] 'The Man of Law's Tale,' 703.

[95] 'The Knight's Tale,' 2511. The Naker was an early timpani-type percussion instrument.

[96] Ibid., 2565.

> Now ryngen trompes loude and clarioun.
> There is namoore to seyn, but west and est
> In goon the speres ful sadly in arrest;
> In gooth the sharpe spore into the syde.
> Ther seen men who kan juste and who kan ryde.[97]

And the winners are greeted by all the wind instrument minstrels in a joyous celebration.

> The trompes, with the loude mynstralcie,
> The heraudes, that ful loude yelle and crie,
> Been in hire wele for joye.[98]

We might mention here that in his poem, 'The Former Age,' Chaucer imagines some former 'blissful life, peaceful and sweet,' where there was no war. Consequently, these people also did not know the trumpets of war.

> No trompes for the werres folk ne knewe.[99]

Music for hunting is also mentioned by Chaucer. In 'The Nun's Priest's Tale,' we read of horns made of brass, wood and bone in which the hunters 'blew and bellowed.'[100] In 'The Book of the Duchess' a specific hunting horn signal is mentioned: 'three mots,' for the uncoupling of the hounds.[101]

The medieval tower watchman-musician, here the 'keeper of the fourth gate,' is also present.[102]

A final form of functional music which Chaucer includes is the bagpipe music of the miller, to which the pilgrims of the 'Canterbury Tales' walk.

> A baggepipe wel koude he blowe and sowne,
> And therwithal he broghte us out of towne.[103]

In ancient and medieval literature the most frequently mentioned form of entertainment music is that performed for the banquet. The reference by Chaucer to 'The mynstralcye, the service at the feeste,'[104] must have been a common occurrence. For a great banquet additional musicians would be needed and it is here we find the wandering jongleurs earning a few coins.

---

97 Ibid., 2600.
98 Ibid., 2671.
99 'The Former Age,' 23.
100 'The Nun's Priest's Tale,' 4588.
101 'The Book of the Duchess,' 375. See also 345.
102 'The Romaunt of the Rose,' 4236ff.
103 'Prologue, The Canterbury Tales,' 564.
104 'The Knight's Tale,' 2197.

> As jogelours pleyen at thise feestes grete.[105]

It was the normal tradition at banquets with important guests to have the food brought out from the kitchen, one course at a time, in a procession led by the wind instrument minstrels. This is exactly what Chaucer mentions in describing a wedding feast.

> Biforn hem stoode instrumentz of swich soun
> That Orpheus, ne of Thebes Amphioun,
> Ne maden nevere swich a melodye.
> At every cours thanne cam loud mynstralcye.[106]

And for entertainment at such banquets, the guests sang and danced.

> There feste they, there daunce they and synge.[107]

---

[105] 'The Squire's Tale,' 219.
[106] 'The Merchant's Tale,' 1715.
[107] 'The Legend of Good Women,' 2157

Leonardo da Vinci on Music

> *Leonardo's performance on the lyre surpassed all musicians of his time.*[1]
>
> Lomazzo, 1590

LEONARDO DA VINCI (1452–1519) was perhaps the most broadly talented man who has yet lived. Apart from his drawings in his notebooks, which include not only virtually every machine known to the fifteenth century (and some not known, such as the helicopter), but also anatomy, zoology, optics and architecture, there is that extraordinary letter of job application which he wrote to Lodovico of Milan. After describing his abilities in designing instruments of war, from special cannons to armor plated vehicles and ships, he added,

> In time of peace I believe that I can give you as complete satisfaction as anyone else in architecture, in the construction of buildings both private and public, and in conducting water from one place to another.
>
> Also I can execute sculpture in marble, bronze, or clay, and also painting, in which my work will stand comparison with that of anyone else whoever he may be.

Were all those skills sufficient to convince Lodovico to hire Leonardo? Apparently not, for according to one sixteenth-century writer, Vasari, it was Leonardo's skill in music which won him the job![2] When he arrived he apparently won great applause by his performance on an instrument he had made, a silver lyre in the shape of a horse's skull.

Another contemporary, Paolo Giovio, reports that Leonardo's performances on the lyre were received by young and old with wonder and delight.[3] A sixteenth-century writer, Lomazzo, reports that his performance on the lyre 'surpassed all musicians of his time.'[4]

As with everything else the man was interested in, Leonardo's interest in music carried him into a study of the most remote corners of the subject, including sketches of numerous inventions and improvements of musical instruments and notes on acoustics. Among these are sketches for means of adding the missing diatonic notes on the trumpet and the problem of making the holes in woodwind instruments where the human hand could reach them. There are also sketches which show him attempting to construct a keyboard for wind instruments.[5]

---

1   Lomazzo, *Idea del Tempio della Pittura* [1590].

2   Quoted in *The Literary Works of Leonardo da Vinci*, ed. Jean Paul Richter (London: Phaidon, 1970), I, 69.

3   Paolo Giovio, *Leonardi Vencii Vita* [1528)].

4   Lomazzo, *Idea del Tempio della Pittura*.

5   Arundel Codex 263.

It is our great loss that Leonardo apparently wrote at least two books on music which are no longer extant. One of these, on the voice, he mentioned in one of his notes.

> My book 'On Voice' is in the hands of Messer Battista dell' Aquila, steward-in-waiting to the pope.[6]

The note which follows this reference mentions a second book, on musical instruments.

> And I shall not enlarge on this as the subject is dealt with very fully in the book on musical instruments.[7]

Of course, if we had these books we would have a priceless source on Renaissance music. Unfortunately, many of the remaining comments on music by Leonardo are clothed in discussion of other arts or are comments used in analogy. His frequent use of music in analogy in itself speaks for the fact that he recognized the universality of music.

We will present the most interesting of these comments by Leonardo we have found for the interest of the reader. We begin with a few of his remarks on other subjects which throw light on his thinking about art or aesthetics, or have some parallel relationship with music.

First, as one can fully understand from looking at even a handful of his sketches made when he was interested in some question, Leonardo placed the highest value on his own personal experience. In this way he was a very modern man; he did not take the Church's word or her pronouncements of faith as a substitute for knowledge based on his own experience. Even more important, with respect to his contrast to earlier philosophers, the senses became the adjudicators of Truth. While the earlier Church scholastic philosophers said, 'you can't trust the senses,' Leonardo said they are the only thing you can trust!

> They say that knowledge born of experience is mechanical, but that knowledge born and consummated in the mind is scientific, while knowledge born of science and culminating in manual work is semi-mechanical. But to me it seems that all sciences are vain and full or errors that are not born of experience, mother of all certainty, and that are not tested by experience, that is to say, that do not at their origin, middle or end pass through any of the five senses. (For if we are doubtful about the certainty of things that pass through the senses how much more should we question the many things against which these senses rebel, such as the nature of God and the soul and the like, about which there are endless disputes and controversies. And truly it so happens that where reason is not, its place is taken by clamor. This never occurs when things are certain. Therefore, where there are quarrels, there true science is not; because truth can only end one way—wherever it is known, controversy is silenced for all time, and should controversy nevertheless again arise, then our conclusions must have been uncertain and confused and not truth which is reborn.) All true sciences are the result of experience which has passed through our senses, thus silencing the tongues of litigants.[8]

---

[6] *The Literary Works of Leonardo da Vinci*, I, 113. Most references in this chapter are taken from this source, which also gives the original library and shelf-marks where the autograph documents may be found.

[7] Ibid., I, 113.

[8] Ibid., I, 33ff.

As one might suspect from so distinguished a painter and sculptor, Leonardo states numerous times that among the senses of man, vision is the most valuable. Hearing comes in second, but only in its role of affirming vision.

> The eye, which is the window of the soul, is the chief organ whereby the understanding can have the most complete and magnificent view of the infinite works of nature; and the ear comes second, which acquires dignity by hearing the things the eye has seen. If you historians, or poets, or mathematicians, had never seen things with your eyes, you could report but imperfectly on them in your writing.[9]

For many centuries philosophers had wondered and argued over the question of the process by which we obtain the information of the senses. In the case of vision, it was clear to Leonardo that we actually capture the image itself. He took as proof of this the example that in looking at a bright light, when we close the eye we can still see the image in the eye.[10] He made no comparable analogy for the sense of hearing, but he did use the illustration of water making circles when a stone is thrown in it as a demonstration of the explanation for the nature of sound waves.[11]

It is also interesting that Leonardo makes another analogy with music in the relationship with the visual perspective of objects as they recede into the distance and the aural perspective of notes as they proceed in time.

> Although the objects seen by the eye do, in fact, touch each other as they recede, I will nevertheless found my rule on spaces of 20 braccia each; as a musician does with notes, which, though they can be carried on one into the next, he divides into degrees from note to note, calling them first, second, third, fourth, fifth; and has affixed a name to each degree in raising or lowering the voice.[12]

Similarly, the Church fathers had for centuries speculated on the location of the soul, an important necessity for a dogma based on life after death. Leonardo, created an analogy in the field of music to demonstrate his conviction that the soul is in the body, but not of the body.

> The soul can never be corrupted with the corruption of the body, but is in the body as it were the air which causes the sound of the organ, where, when a pipe bursts, the wind would cease to have any good effect.[13]

Leonardo's faith in his own learning from experience also colored his views on education. First of all, the cost and effort of higher education was, he felt, something which was simply not appropriate to the average man.

---

[9] Ibid., I, 56, 367.

[10] Ibid., I, 132.

[11] Ibid., I, 140.

[12] Ibid., I, 157.

[13] Ibid., II, 238.

> It seems to me that men of coarse and clumsy habits and of small knowledge do not deserve such fine instruments or so great a variety of natural mechanism as men of speculation and of great knowledge ... for it seems to me they have nothing about them of the human species but the voice and the figure, and for all the rest are much below beasts.[14]

And again, education had no value unless it occurred from direct experience. Rote teaching and presenting conclusions to the students was not education of the person.

> Any one who in discussion relies upon authority uses, not his understanding, but rather his memory.[15]

With regard to the ancient traditional education, Leonardo several times mentioned his sensitivity to the fact that painting was not considered a member of the liberal arts.

> Painting has every right to complain of being driven out from the number of Liberal Arts, since she is a true daughter of nature and employs the noblest of all the senses. It was wrong, oh [ancient] writers, to leave her out from the number of Liberal Arts, because she deals not only with the works of nature but extends over an infinite number of things which nature never created.[16]

Leonardo was perhaps the first important artist who talked about what we call today Expressionism, painting not merely the physical resemblance of the man, but painting what the man is thinking.

> The good painter must paint principally two things, which are man and the ideas in man's mind. The first is easy, the second difficult, because they can only be expressed by means of gestures and the movements of the limbs.[17]

Above all in this regard, Leonardo was thinking of expressing the emotions of the subject and he advised the young artists to observe and take notes on the faces they see of persons expressing various emotions. He makes the additional remarkable recommendation that they study the dumb, who can express their emotions only by face and gesture, without the aid of the voice.[18]

On the subject of the emotions, Leonardo's most vivid comments on emotions are all limited to pain.

> Pleasure and Pain represent twins, since there never is one without the other; and as if they were united back to back, since they are contrary to each other.

---

[14] Ibid., II, 235.

[15] Ibid., II, 241.

[16] Ibid., I, 67.

[17] Quoted in Anthony Blunt, *Artistic Theory in Italy, 1450–1600* (Oxford: Clarendon Press, 1959), 34. A nice definition of the conductor, as well!

[18] Quoted in Ibid., 35.

> If you take Pleasure know that he has behind him one who will deal you Tribulation and Repentance.[19]

Still other comments appear very personal, as,

> The tears come from the heart and not from the brain.[20]

Leonardo wrote frequently of beauty as found in nature, but he does not attempt to define it as a philosopher might. For him it seems to have been sufficient to recognize that beauty was of the realm of the artist. Here was his opportunity to argue against the members of liberal arts, which had omitted painting. 'Art,' he says, 'is not like mathematics, which one can learn by sheer application.' And of geometry and arithmetic in particular, he observed,

> these two sciences only extend to a knowledge of quantity … but they do not concern themselves with quality, which forms the beauty of the works of nature and the glory of the world.[21]

To this he added one clear definition of Beauty, one of the traditional definitions of high art, that it can have no purpose.

> Beauty and utility cannot exist together, as seen in fortresses and in men.[22]

Leonardo made extensive notes on the ancient question regarding the obligation of art to imitate nature. He seems to have come down rather firmly on the side of the affirmative, primarily because he viewed nature as the ideal which could not be improved upon. It follows, he said, 'That painting is the most to be praised which agrees most exactly with the thing imitated.'[23] Even the ugly, in the painting of a body, should be included, for it serves to point up the beautiful with greater intensity.[24]

On the other hand, he writes in one place that the artist is not merely a scientist who copies nature, but is a creator. Through imitation the artist's mind takes on,

> that divine power, which lies in the knowledge of the painter, transforms the mind of the painter into the likeness of the divine mind, for with a free hand he can produce [that which does not actually exist, including] different beings, animals, plants, fruits, landscapes, open fields, abysses, terrifying and fearful places.[25]

---

19 *The Literary Works of Leonardo da Vinci*, I, 385.

20 Ibid., II, 93. Found together with notes on anatomy!

21 Quoted in Blunt, *Artistic Theory in Italy*, 36.

22 Ibid., II, 359.

23 Quoted in Blunt, *Artistic Theory in Italy*, 30.

24 Quoted in Ibid., 31.

25 Quoted in Ibid., 37.

It is a great virtue of painting, according to Leonardo, that it not only imitates beauty in nature, but preserves its image forever, 'which Nature with all its force could not keep.'

> How many paintings have preserved the image of divine beauty of which time or sudden death have destroyed Nature's original, so that the work of the painter has survived in nobler form that that of Nature, his mistress.[26]

Leonardo also raised the question of the imitation of nature in a very interesting discussion of the study process of the young artist.

> The Adversary says that to acquire practice and do a great deal of work it is better that the first period of study should be employed in copying various compositions ... by diverse masters ... I reply that the method will be good, if it is based on works of good composition and by skilled masters. But since such masters are so rare that there are but few of them to be found, it is a surer way to go to natural objects than to those which are imitated from nature with great deterioration, and so form bad methods;[27] for he who can go to the fountain does not go to the water-jar.[28]

An especially interesting reference to the imitation of nature has to do with the imitation of emotions, 'That figure is most admirable which by its actions best expresses the emotions [*la passione*] that animates it.'[29] We get some idea how vividly he meant this in a passage in which he speaks of painting a hypothetical battle scene.

> Others must be represented in the agonies of death grinding their teeth, rolling their eyes, with their fists clenched against their bodies and their legs contorted.[30]

On a related topic, he recommends that 'the motions of men must be such as suggest their dignity or their baseness.'[31]

The skill, or craft, of the artist, in Leonardo's view, was first based on experience, and as anyone knows who has seen the meticulous notes and drawings of Leonardo's sketchbooks, his concept of experience included the most precise discipline of observation. From experience comes the knowledge and rules of the craft.

> Good [artistic] judgment is born of clear understanding, and a clear understanding comes of reasons derived from sound rules, and sound rules are the product of sound experience—the common mother of all the sciences and arts.[32]

......

---

[26] *The Literary Works of Leonardo da Vinci*, I, 77.

[27] We were once told by a music educator that one should purposely give students some bad compositions to play, for how else would they learn what good compositions were!

[28] *The Literary Works of Leonardo da Vinci*, I, 305.

[29] Ibid., I, 341.

[30] Ibid., I, 349.

[31] Ibid., I, 346.

[32] Ibid., I, 119.

> Those who devote themselves to practice without science are like sailors who put to sea without rudder or compass and who can never be certain where they are going. Practice must always be founded on sound theory.[33]

Leonardo gave more space to defining the concept that art is found in the mind of the artist and not in the work of his hands.

Finally, Leonardo included in his notes a little joke he no doubt used with his students when talking about the imitation of nature.

> A painter was asked why, since he made such beautiful figures ... his children were so ugly; to which the painter replied that he made his pictures by day, and his children by night.[34]

Another attractive story on this theme relates to his most famous painting, *The Last Supper*. Leonardo had essentially finished the work except for the head of Judas. He was much troubled about what kind of face would be appropriate for this man for whom so much of the world held such hatred. He walked around the poorest, most destitute areas of Milan, sketching the faces of the ugly and miserable men he found there. But he could not find a face that seemed appropriate. All this time a clerical busy-body was going back and forth from the workshop to the duke, complaining that Leonardo wasn't working, that he just was sitting around. Then he would return conveying the duke's order that Leonardo must complete the painting, etc. Finally Leonardo was exasperated and painted the face of the clerical busy-body as the head of Judas!

In one of the many places where Leonardo argued for recognition of the art of painting he sets out to prove that painting is a higher art than poetry. Following a nice play on words, he again calls upon music in analogy.

> Painting is poetry which is seen and not heard, and poetry is a painting which is heard but not seen. These two arts, you may call them both either poetry or painting, have here interchanged the senses by which they penetrate to the intellect. Whatever is painted must pass by the eye, which is the nobler sense, and whatever is poetry must pass through a less noble sense, namely, the ear, to the understanding.[35]

He observed that the eye can immediately take in an entire painting, while in poetry the listener must follow a long series of individual details before understanding the whole. This Leonardo compared to hearing separate lines of music without hearing them performed together.

---

33 Quoted in Blunt, *Artistic Theory in Italy*, 28.

34 *The Literary Works of Leonardo da Vinci*, II, 289.

35 Ibid., I, 58ff.

> The poet's way may be compared to that of a musician who all by himself undertakes to sing a composition which is intended for four voices and first sings the part of the soprano, then that of the tenor, then the contralto, and finally the bass. Such performances cannot produce the beauty of harmonious proportions set in harmonious divisions of time.[36]

It is interesting that one of his arguments was that painting has the power to arouse stronger emotions than poetry. This he found particularly true in the example of love, which he declared is 'the main motive of the species in the whole animal world.' He offers as a demonstration of proof the following anecdote.

> It once happened to me that I made a picture representing a sacred subject which was bought by one who loved it and who then wished to remove the symbols of divinity in order that he might kiss her without misgivings. Finally his conscience prevailed over his sighs and lust and he felt constrained to remove the picture from his house. Now let the poet go and try to rouse such desires in men by the description of a beauty which does not portray any living being.[37]

Leonardo also sought to make the case that painting is a higher art than sculpture, pointing out that the sculptor does not have to deal with color or such problems as foreshortening. However, in a rare humorous passage, Leonardo admits that the physical work of the sculptor is more difficult. Again he refers to music.

> The sculptor in carving his statue out of marble or other stone wherein it is potentially contained has to take off the superfluous and excessive parts with the strength of his arms and the strokes of the hammer—a very mechanical exercise causing much perspiration which mingling with the grit turns into mud. His face is pasted and smeared all over with marble powder, making him look like a baker …
> How different the painter's lot … for the painter sits in front of his work at perfect ease. He is well dressed and handles a light brush dipped in delightful color. He is arrayed in the garments he fancies, and his home is clean and filled with delightful pictures, and he often enjoys the accompaniment of music.[38]

In fact, Vasari reports that Leonardo painted his famous *Mona Lisa* to the accompaniment of music.[39]

In view of the fact that Leonardo was reported to be a skilled and sensitive musician, it strikes the reader as very odd that his voice is not found joining the humanists in praise of the virtues of music. Instead, in his notes we find him focusing on the deficiencies of music as an art—for the purpose, as in the case of poetry and sculpture, of pointing to the superiority of painting.

---

[36] Ibid., I, 60, 79.

[37] Ibid., I, 64.

[38] Ibid., I, 91.

[39] Ibid., I, 72.

The first deficiency of music, in his view, was that it was associated with one of the senses which he believed inferior to vision. In particular, he observed that the ear lacks the accuracy of sight.

> But the ear is apt to be misled in locating and judging the distances of its objects because the lines along which sound travels are not straight like those of the pyramid of sight, but tortuous and bent. And very often distant sounds seem nearer than those close by, owing to the transmission; although the sound of the echo travels to the ear by straight lines only.[40]

Therefore it follows, as he wrote in several places, to be born blind is a much greater loss than to be born deaf.

> He who is born blind cannot replace this experience through the sense of hearing because he has never known what is the beauty of anything. There remains to him the sense of hearing whereby he hears [only] the voices and the speech of men which is composed of the names of all things that have been given names. But one can live happily without the knowledge of these names as is shown by those born deaf, who, being dumb, make themselves understood by drawing, which most of them enjoy.[41]
>
> ......
>
> Who would not lose his sense of hearing and the senses of smell and touch as well rather than his sight, because he who loses his sight is like a man chased from the world—for he no longer sees it nor anything of it, and such life is the sister of death.[42]
>
> ......
>
> There is nobody so senseless who when given the choice of either remaining in perpetual darkness or losing his hearing will not at once say that he prefers to lose his hearing and his sense of smell as well rather than be blind. Because whoever loses his eyesight loses the beauty of the world with all the forms in creation, whereas deafness only brings the loss of sound, caused by motion arising from the percussion of the air, which is a very small matter.[43]

The second fundamental deficiency of music, which Leonardo found, was that it does not last, it disappears. This was an argument mentioned by a number of ancient Greek philosophers, as he had no doubt become aware through the general interest of the fifteenth-century humanists in ancient literature.

> And from these shapes is born the proportionality called harmony, which delights the sense of sight with sweet concord just as the proportions of diverse voices delight the sense of hearing. But the harmony of music is less noble than the harmony which appeals to the eye, because the sound dies as soon as it is born, and its death is as swift as its birth, and this cannot happen with the sense of sight. For if you present to the eye the beauty of a human figure composed of fine proportions, these beau-

---

[40] Ibid., I, 38ff.

[41] Ibid., I, 39.

[42] Ibid., I, 40.

[43] Ibid., I, 66.

> ties will not be as transient nor will they be destroyed as swiftly as in music. On the contrary, beauty has a long life; it can be enjoyed and examined at leisure without having to be continually reborn like music which has to be played again and again, and it will not weary you …[44]
>
> ……
>
> Music cannot be called otherwise than the sister of painting, for she is dependent upon hearing, a sense second to sight, and her harmony is composed of the union of its proportional parts sounded simultaneously, rising and falling in one or more harmonic rhythms. These rhythms may be said to surround the proportionality of the members composing the harmony, just as the contour bounds the members from which human beauty is born.
>
> But painting excels and ranks higher than music, because it does not fade away as soon as it is born, as is the fate of unhappy music.[45]
>
> …..
>
> Music has two ills, one of which is mortal, and the other subjects it to deterioration. The mortal is ever linked to the instant which follows its creation, while the deterioration lies in its repetition making it hateful and vile.[46]

He must have known, but neglected to mention, that the ancient Greek philosophers held music to be a higher art than painting, which was relegated to the crafts such as carpentry. The Greeks held music in high estate in part because you cannot *see* music, hence they found it had a certain mystery similar to religion. Leonardo did mention this last aspect of music in passing.

> The poet ranks far below the painter in the representation of visible things, and far below the musician in that of invisible things.[47]

Leonardo also argued that for the true portrayal of Nature, painting, and not music, is the appropriate art.

> It is a sin against nature to want to give to the ear what is meant for the eye. Let music enter there and do not try to put in her place the science of painting, the true imitator of all the shapes of nature.[48]

In view of these arguments which he believed demonstrated the inferiority of music to painting, Leonardo could not understand why music was admitted as a member of the Liberal Arts, while painting was not. Here we see clearly the degree to which he had a chip on his shoulder.

> After giving a place to Music among the Liberal Arts you must place Painting there, too, or else withdraw Music.[49]

---

[44] Ibid., I, 61.

[45] Ibid., I, 76.

[46] Ibid., II, 233.

[47] Ibid., I, 80.

[48] Ibid., I, 62.

[49] Ibid., I, 79.

Among all the extensive autograph notes and letters by Leonardo, there is not a single reference to an actual performance of music which he heard. We are left with only a few clues from which to deduce his thoughts on performance. One of his notes, for example, seems to be an oblique reference to performers who were not fulfilling their duties as he understood it.

> And if you say that there are vile painters, I reply that Music also can be spoiled by those who do not understand it.[50]

In another case, in speaking of how the eye takes in an entire painting at once, Leonardo provides another analogy with music. Here he reveals a striking awareness of the power of music and the experience of the contemplative listener.

> And from painting which serves the eye, the noblest sense, arises harmony of proportions; just as many different voices joined together and singing simultaneously produce a harmonious proportion which gives such satisfaction to the sense of hearing that the listeners remain spellbound with admiration as if half alive.[51]

---

[50] Ibid., I, 79.

[51] Ibid., I, 59.

Baldassare Castiglione on Music

Baldassare Castiglione (1478–1529), as a diplomat for the Duke of Urbino and Popes Leo X and Clement VII, had the opportunity to observe Italian culture at its highest level. From this experience came one of the most famous books of the Renaissance, *Il Cortigiano* (*The Courtier*), which attempts to describe the attributes of the perfect gentleman[1] and lady from the sixteenth century perspective. In spite of some very modern goals for his perfect gentleman, Castiglione remained in some ways an old fashioned Church philosopher, as is especially reflected in his views on women and on the relationship of Reason and the emotions.

Castiglione's ideal man, the *l'uomo universale*, must be noble born, skilled and learned in virtually all fields, gentle, sensitive and tactful. In the spirit of the latter, Castiglione says he has tried to use language which is graceful, euphonious, valid and expressive.[2] He also promises us the truth, for as a 'worthless painter,' Castiglione says he lacks the skill to 'adorn the truth with pretty colors or use perspective to deceive the eye.'

His book, which presents a discussion on the definition of the perfect gentleman by a group of nobles, is dedicated to a young courtier 'of perfect behavior and proficient in everything,' Alfonso Ariosto, who died at a young age. 'Fortune,' says Castiglione, 'hasn't changed her ways: she still hates virtue as much as she ever did.'[3]

With regard to music, Castiglione presents an extensive argument for the true gentleman being, in addition to everything else, a musician. This remarkable passage speaks of the gentleman not only being expected to read at sight, but play several instruments. He goes on to praise the various virtues of music found in ancient literature and mentions its purposes. The Count, begins,

> 'Gentlemen, I must tell you that I am not satisfied with our courtier unless he is also a musician and unless as well as understanding and being able to read music he can play several instruments. For, when we think of it, during our leisure time we can find nothing more worthy or commendable to help our bodies relax and our spirits recuperate, especially at Court where, besides the way in which music helps everyone to forget his troubles, many things are done to please the ladies, whose tender and gentle souls are very susceptible to harmony and sweetness. So it is no wonder that both in ancient times and today they have always been extremely fond of musicians and have welcomed music as true refreshment for the spirit.'
>
> Signor Gaspare commented: 'I think that music, like so many other vanities, is most certainly very suited to women, and perhaps also to some of those who have the appearance of men, but not to real men who should not indulge in pleasures which render their minds effeminate and so cause them to fear death.'

---

[1] *The Courtier*, II, 145ff, trans. George Bull (New York: Penguin Books, 1967.

[2] Ibid., Prologue, 34. Citations will give the Book number of the original, in addition to the page number from this edition.

[3] Ibid., Prologue, 32.

'Do not say that,' retorted the Count, 'or I shall launch into oceans of praise for music and remind you how greatly it was honored in the ancient world, and held to be sacred, and that the wisest of philosophers held the opinion that the universe was made up of music, that the heavens make harmony as they move, and that as our own souls are formed on the same principle they are awakened and have their faculties, as it were, brought to life thorough music. And because of this it is recorded that Alexander was sometimes so stirred by music that almost against his will under its influence he was constrained to rise from the banquet table and rush to arms; then the musician would play something different, and growing calmer he would return from arms to the banquet. And, let me also tell you, grave Socrates, when he was already very old, learned to play the cithara. Moreover, I remember having heard that Plato and Aristotle insist that a well-educated man should also be a musician; and with innumerable arguments they show that music exerts a powerful influence on us, and, for many reasons that would take too long to explain, they say that it has to be learned in childhood, not so much for the sake of its audible melodies but because of its capacity to breed good new habits and a virtuous disposition and make the soul more receptive to happiness, just as exercise makes the body more robust; and they add that music far from being harmful to the pursuits of peace or war is greatly to their benefit. Then again, in the stern laws which he made, Lycurgus gave his approval to music. And we read that in battle the bellicose Spartans and Cretans used citharas and other sweet-sounding instruments; and that many outstanding commanders of the ancient world, such as Epaminondas, practiced music, and those who were ignorant of music, such as Themistocles, were far less respected. Have you not heard, as well, that among the first subjects which the good Chiron taught to the young Achilles was music, and that this wise and venerable teacher wished the hands that were to shed so much Trojan blood often to be employed in playing the cithara? What kind of warrior, then, would be ashamed to follow the example of Achilles, let alone all the other famous commanders whom I could cite? So you must not wish to deprive our courtier of music, which not only soothes the souls of men but often tames wild beasts. Indeed, the man who does not enjoy music can be sure that there is no harmony in his soul. And remember that it has such powers that once it caused a fish to let itself be ridden by a man over the tempestuous sea. We see it used in sacred places to render praise and thanks to God; and we may well believe that it is agreeable to God, and that He has given it to us as a soothing balm for our toils and tribulations. Thus common laborers in the field working under the burning sun will often relieve their tedium with simple country songs. And the ordinary peasant girl, rising before dawn to spin or weave, uses music to ward off sleep and make her work agreeable; distressed mariners, after the rains and the winds and the storms, love to relax with the help of music; weary pilgrims find solace in music on their long and exhausting journey, as so often do chained and fettered prisoners in their misery. As even stronger evidence that even the most unsophisticated melodies lighten the burden of all our toils and tribulations in this world, we find that Nature herself has taught it to the nurse as the sure way to still the persistent crying of young babies, who are lulled to quiet rest and sleep by the sound of her singing, forgetting the tears which at that age are right and proper as a presage of our later life.'

After the Count had been silent for a moment, the Magnifico Giuliano[4] said: 'I am not at all of the same opinion of signor Gaspare; on the contrary, for the reasons you have given and for many others besides, I believe that music is not only an ornament but a necessity for the courtier. However, I should like you to explain how he is to practice this and the other accomplishments that you assign to him, and on what occasions and in what manner; for there are many things which in themselves

---

4 Giuliano de Medici (1479–1516), brother to Pope Leo X, he led a dissolute life. Nevertheless, his portrait was painted by Raphael and he was the subject of a sculpture by Michelangelo.

are commendable but which are most unseemly when practiced at the wrong time; and on the other hand, there are many things that seem inconsequential but which are greatly esteemed when performed on the appropriate occasion.'[5]

Castiglione does not elaborate further here, but in his account of the following day he has Federico add,

> I think the courtier should possess good judgment, the need for which was rightly mentioned by the Count yesterday evening. If he does have it, then he needs no other instructions about how to practice what he knows at the right time and in the proper manner. To attempt to provide him with more precise rules would be too difficult and surely superfluous. For I do not know who would be so inept as to want to take up arms when others are attending to music; or to do a Morris dance in the streets,[6] no matter how good he is at it; or comfort a mother for the loss of her son by laughing and joking. I'm sure no gentleman would do such things, unless he were completely out of his wits.[7]

In addition to the purposes of music given in the above, in another place we find one not previously mentioned in early literature.

> … like children in the dark singing to themselves to pluck up courage, as if they were driving away their fears with song.[8]

In the lengthy discussion of music above, we have seen the Count argue that every gentleman must be a performing musician, and the Magnifico Giuliano call music 'a necessity for the courtier.' These views, however, may have been included by Castiglione for the purpose of representing another point of view, for they are somewhat in conflict with his fundamental attitude toward a gentleman's activities. While Castiglione gives abundant evidence that the gentleman should appreciate listening to music, being a skilled performer was quite another matter. Basically, Castiglione believed the gentleman should display a certain nonchalance about all skills and should not be expected to apply himself in any form of hard labor which might result in excellence in any skill. For example, he calls chess a refined recreation, but for the defect that it demands so much knowledge. Since this requires much time and study, he concludes that, with regard to being a chess player, 'mediocrity is more to be praised than excellence.'[9] Likewise, he recommends tennis as a game worthy of the courtier, but he cautions,

---

[5] Ibid., I, 94ff.

[6] In another place, Ibid., II, 117, Castiglione says 'a gentleman should never honor by his personal appearance a country show, where the spectators and participants are common people.'

[7] Ibid., II, 112ff.

[8] Ibid., II, 124.

[9] Ibid., II, 140.

> Even though his performance is outstanding, he should not let it be thought that he has spent on it much time and trouble. Neither should he behave like those people who are fond of music and, whenever they are speaking with someone, if there is a lull in the conversation always start to sing *sotto voce*.[10]

His basic contention seems to be that 'affectation,' being an enthusiast of, or expert in, any activity deprives one's performance of grace, and that the highest form of grace is simplicity and nonchalance.

> Leaving aside those who are endowed with [grace] by their stars, I have discovered a universal rule which seems to apply more than any other in all human actions or words: namely, to steer away from affectation at all costs, as if it were a rough and dangerous reef and to practice in all things a certain nonchalance which conceals all artistry and makes whatever one says or does seem uncontrived and effortless. I am sure that grace springs especially from this, since everyone knows how difficult it is to accomplish some unusual feat perfectly, and so facility in such things excites the greatest wonder; whereas, in contrast, to labor at what one is doing and, as we say, to make bones over it, shows an extreme lack of grace and causes everything, whatever its worth, to be discounted. So we can truthfully say that true art is what does not seem to be art; and the most important thing is to conceal it, because if it is revealed this discredits a man completely and ruins his reputation.[11]

He cites here ancient orators who purposely tried to hide their skills, for if the populace perceived their true skills they would be frightened of being deceived.

In another place he claims that it was believed among great painters of the ancient world that excessive diligence is harmful. He mentions in particular an ancient painter, Protogenes, who did not know when to stop and was blamed for finishing his work too thoroughly. Castiglione then continues,

> So this quality which is the opposite of affectation, and which we are now calling nonchalance, apart from being the real source of grace, brings with it another advantage; for whatever action it accompanies, no matter how trivial it is, it not only reveals the skill of the person doing it but also very often causes it to be considered far greater than it really is. This is because it makes the onlookers believe that a man who performs well with so much facility must possess even greater skill than he does, and that if he took great pains and effort he would perform even better.[12]

In this regard he gives the example of a musician. This comment is especially valuable as proof that the so-called 'Baroque cadenza' was already common in the sixteenth century.

> When a musician is singing and utters a single word ending in a group of notes with a sweet cadence, and with such ease that it seems effortless, that touch alone proves that he is capable of far more than he is doing.

---

[10] Ibid., II, 118.

[11] Ibid., I, 67.

[12] Ibid., I, 69ff.

Later, Castiglione returns to the attitude of nonchalance which the gentleman must exhibit relative to his own performance as a musician. The subject is introduced by Federico.

> 'For there is nothing so perfect in the world that the ignorant do not tire of it and despise it when they see it often. My judgment is the same with regard to music. Thus I should not like our courtier to behave as do so many others as soon as they put in an appearance, even in the presence of gentlemen who are strangers to them, immediately, hardly waiting to be asked, start showing off what they know, and often what they don't know, in such a way that it seems that they have come along just for this purpose and that it is their main pursuit in life. So the courtier should turn to music as if it were merely a pastime of his and he is yielding to persuasion, and not in the presence of common people or a large crowd. And although he may know and understand what he is doing, in this also I wish him to dissimulate the care and effort that are necessary for any competent performance; and he should let it seem as if he himself thinks nothing of his accomplishment which, because of its excellence, he makes others think very highly of.'[13]

Castiglione in numerous places treats the gentlewoman as distinctly disadvantaged as compared to the gentleman.[14] From this it followed that she should not engage in the activities of the gentleman, such as playing tennis for example. She was for this reason more limited in her opportunities as a musician.

> For example, when she is dancing I should not wish to see her use movements that are too forceful and energetic, nor, when she is singing or playing a musical instrument, to use those abrupt and frequent *diminuendos* that are ingenious but not beautiful. And I suggest that she should choose instruments suited to her purpose. Imagine what an ungainly sight it would be to have a woman playing drums, fifes, trumpets or other instruments of that sort; and this is simply because their stridency buries and destroys the sweet gentleness which embellished everything a woman does.[15]

In only one place does Castiglione offer details of actual musical materials, but it is an interesting passage, used for the purpose of illustrating the principle that nonchalance carried to an extreme is a fault.

> It certainly holds true in music, in which it is very wrong to have two perfect consonances one after the other; for our sense of hearing abhors this, whereas it often likes a second or a seventh, which in itself is a harsh and unbearable discord. This is because to continue in perfect consonances produces satiety and offers a harmony which is too affected; but this disappears when imperfect consonances are introduced to establish the contrast which keeps the listener in a state of expectancy, waiting for and enjoying the perfect consonances more eagerly and delighting in the discord of the second or seventh, as in a display of nonchalance.[16]

---

[13] Ibid., II, 120.

[14] On the inferiority of women, see Ibid., II, 201. He does acknowledge that in earlier times there had been women who were 'very talented in music, painting and sculpture.' [Ibid., III, 240] An even more interesting observation is made by Giuliano de Medici, that 'there can be no doubt that being weaker in body women are abler in mind and more capable of speculative thought than men.' [Ibid., III, 218]

[15] Ibid., III, 215.

[16] Ibid., I, 69.

Castiglione provides lengthy descriptions of an environment of art music among the aristocracy of sixteenth-century Italy. He sets the stage for these comments by describing an ideal palace, that of Duke Federico of Urbino, which is adorned 'with the usual objects, such as silver vases, wall-hangings of the richest cloth of gold, silk and other similar material,' but also countless antique statues of marble and bronze, valuable paintings and 'every kind of musical instrument.'[17] He also mentions 'musical performances' in a list of activities appropriate to the well-born gentlemen of this court.[18] In the rooms of the duchess as well, the activities include 'constant music and dancing.' Therefore, he concludes, in this court were to be found 'poets, musicians, buffoons of all kinds, and the finest talent of every description anywhere in Italy.'

Castiglione displays his disdain for the man who will not listen to music, and thus has no place in court, in the following anecdote about a courtier whom a lady had asked to dance,

> and who not only refused but would not listen to music or take part in the many other entertainments offered, protesting all the while that such frivolities were not his business. And when at length the lady asked what his business was, he answered with a scowl: 'Fighting …'
>
> 'Well then,' the lady retorted, 'I should think that since you aren't at war at the moment and you are not engaged in fighting, it would be a good thing if you were to have yourself well greased and stowed away in a cupboard with all your fighting equipment, so that you avoid getting rustier than you are already.'
>
> And of course everyone burst out laughing at the way she showed her contempt for his stupid presumption.[19]

Castiglione, in making the point that each artist has his own personal style and therefore dissimilar styles can merit equal praise, provides us with a valuable portrait of the sixteenth-century Italian singer of art song. That this is art music is clearly evidenced by the impact on the contemplative listeners.

> In music, for example, the strains are now solemn and slow, now very fast and different in mood and manner. Yet the performance is always agreeable, though for varying reasons. For example, Bidon's style of singing is so skillful, quick, vehement and passionate, and of such melodious variety, that the spirits of those listening are excited and aroused, and feel so exalted that they seem to be drawn up to heaven. Then the singing of our own Marchetto Cara is just as moving, but its harmonies are softer; his voice is serene and so full of plaintive sweetness that he gently touches and penetrates our souls, and they respond with great delight and emotion.[20]

Later we find an extraordinary and extensive discussion of aesthetics in art music, introduced by Gaspare.

> 'There exist many different kinds of music, both vocal and instrumental. So I would be gratified to hear which is the best of all and on what occasion the courtier should perform.'

---

[17] Ibid., I, 41.

[18] Ibid., I, 42, 44.

[19] Ibid., I, 58.

[20] Ibid., I, 82.

'Truly beautiful music,' answered Federico, 'consists, in my opinion, in fine singing, in reading accurately from the score and in an attractive personal style, and still more in singing to the accompaniment of the viol. I say this because the solo voice contains all the purity of music, and style and melody are studied and appreciated more carefully when our ears are not distracted by more than one voice, and every little fault, too, is more clearly apparent, something which does not happen when a group is singing, because then one singer covers up for the other. But above all, singing poetry accompanied by the viol seems especially pleasurable, for the instrument gives the words a really marvelous charm and effectiveness. All keyboard instruments, indeed, are harmonious, because their consonances are perfect and they make possible many effects which fill the soul with sweetness and melody. And no less delightful is the playing of a quartet, with the viols producing music of great skill and suavity. The human voice adds ornament and grace to all these instruments, with which I think it is good enough if our courtier has some acquaintance (though the more proficient he is the better) without concerning himself greatly with [the aulos] which both Minerva and Alcibiades rejected, because it seems [to] have something repulsive about [it]. Then as to the occasions when these various kinds of music should be performed, I would instance when a man finds himself in the company of dear and familiar friends, and there is no pressing business on hand. But above all, the time is appropriate when there are ladies present; for the sight of them softens the hearts of those who are listening, makes them more susceptible to the sweetness of the music, and also quickens the spirit of the musicians themselves. As I have already said, one should avoid playing in the presence of a large number, especially of the common people. But in any case, everything should be tempered by discretion; for it is just not possible to imagine all the circumstances possible, and if the courtier is a good judge of himself he will adapt himself to the occasion and will know when his audience is in the mood to listen and when not; and he will act his own age, for it is certainly most unbecoming and unsightly when an old grey-haired gentleman, who is toothless and wrinkled, takes up the viol and plays and sings in front of a gathering of ladies, even if his performance is quite good. This is because the words of songs are nearly always amorous, and in old men love is altogether ridiculous; although it sometimes seems that Cupid along with the other miracles he works delights in melting even the icy hearts of the old.'

Then the Magnifico replied: 'Do not rob such poor old men of this pleasure, Federico; for I have known men of advanced years who possess the most perfect voices and are accomplished musicians, and far more so than some young men.'

'It is not my wish,' answered Federico, 'to rob them of this pleasure, but it certainly is my wish to rob you and these ladies of the chance to laugh at their absurdity; and if old men have the desire to sing to the viol, then let them do so in private with the object of shedding from their minds the disturbing thoughts and bitter vexations of which life is full, and of tasting the divinity which, I believe, Pythagoras and Socrates attributed to music. And even if they do not practice it themselves, if they have cultivated a taste for music they will enjoy it far more than those who know nothing about it. After all, very often, because he exercises them a great deal, a blacksmith whose body is otherwise puny will have stronger arms than someone who is more robust; likewise, someone whose ears have been trained to listen to harmony will understand it better and more readily and appreciate it more intelligently than others whose hearing may be very sharp and sound but whose ears are untrained in the varieties of musical consonances; for the modulations of music have no significance for ears that are unaccustomed to them, though admittedly music can tame even a wild animal. This, then, is the pleasure that old men may suitably take in music.'[21]

---

21   Ibid., II, 120ff

This fascinating passage provides us with such important specific aesthetic values in music from the perspective of the sixteenth-century Italian noble that we should like to summarize them. First, that the highest aesthetic in art music is fine singing, reading from score and with an attractive personal style.

Second, performance mediums are clearly ranked with regard to aesthetics, the highest being solo singing, keyboard playing and chamber music. The aulos, the most important instrument of the ancient world, now is mentioned as a curiosity.

Third, Castiglione makes a passing negative reference to polyphony, representing a characteristic view of Italian humanists and of the sixteenth century in general. He mentions this in another place, where, in speaking of friendship,[22] Castiglione says it is dangerous to have more than two real friends. 'The reason for this is that, as you know, harmony is more difficult to achieve with several instruments than with two.'

Fourth, we are also given the most aesthetic environment for art music: a relaxed atmosphere, when no one has pressing business at hand, when the listeners are in the proper mood, and when ladies are present.

Five, these should be private performances, not before large audiences or the common people.

Closely related to the objection, in the above discussion, to older men being public performers, Castiglione mentions again the unsuitability of old men making music, here recommending they should not actually perform but only give advice and teach.

> Then if the courtier should be so old that it is unbecoming to him to indulge in music, merrymaking, games, arms and similar recreations, even so one cannot say that it is impossible for him to win his prince's favor in this way. For even if he is too old to take part in these things himself, he can still understand them; and, given that he has practiced them when young, seeing that years and experience bring with them so much more knowledge of everything, age does not prevent his having a more perfect judgment, and a more perfect understanding of how to teach them to his prince.[23]

And finally, the misinformed view that one can only appreciate music if one has 'cultivated a taste' for it, or is a trained listener. This is disproved by the simple fact that everyone in the world is prepared by genetics to appreciate music, while few are knowledgeable listeners. We see the other side of this coin, where knowledge can adversely affect the listener, in the following where Castiglione is speaking of the dangers of relying on the opinions of others.

> And to prove this, consider that not so long ago, when certain verses were presented here as being by Sannazaro, everyone thought they were extremely fine and praised them to the skies, then when it was established that they were by someone else their reputation sank immediately and they seemed

---

[22] Ibid., II, 138.

[23] Ibid., IV, 320.

quite mediocre. Then again, when a motet was sung in the presence of the Duchess, it pleased no one and was considered worthless, until it became known that it had been composed by Josquin des Pres.[24]

Castiglione introduces the topic of entertainment by stipulating that even in these circumstances the proper gentleman must maintain grace and discretion.

> I would like the courtier sometimes to descend to calmer and more restful games, and to escape envy and enter pleasantly into the company of all the others by doing everything they do; although he should never fail to behave in a commendable manner and should rule all his actions with that good judgment which will not allow him to take part in any foolishness. Let him laugh, jest, banter, romp and dance, though in a fashion that always reflects good sense and discretion, and let him say and do everything with grace.[25]

Under the general subject of appropriate court entertainment, Castiglione presents a very lengthy discussion of humor. We find particularly interesting the following introduction to the topic of laughter.

> I shall say, as briefly as I can, whatever occurs to me on the subject of the causes of laughter, which is so natural to mankind that to define a man it is customary to say that he is an animal capable of laughing. For laughter is seen only in men, and it is nearly always the sign of a certain inward hilarity of the spirit, which is naturally attracted to pleasure and desirous of rest and recreation. So we see many things devised by men for this purpose, such as festivals and various kinds of spectacle. And because we like those who are responsible for providing us with our recreations, the kings of the ancient world, the Roman, the Athenian and many others, in order to secure the goodwill of the populace and to feed the eyes and mind of the multitude, used to build great theaters and other public edifices, and there they would show new kinds of sport, horse and chariot races, combats, strange beasts, comedies, tragedies and mime. Nor were grave philosophers adverse to such displays, and they would often, both at spectacles of that kind or at banquets, relax their minds which were weary from their exalted discourses and inspired thoughts; and this is something all kinds and conditions of men willingly do, for not only laborers in the fields, sailors and all those who do hard and rough work with their hands but also holy men of religion and prisoners waiting in hourly expectation of death, all seek solace in light recreation. Therefore everything which provokes laugher exalts a man's spirit and gives him pleasure, and for a while enables him to forget the trials and tribulations of which life is full.[26]

On the subject of laughter, Castiglione hastily adds that to *cause* laughter is not appropriate to the gentleman, but rather the fool, drunkard, 'stupid clowns and buffoons.' Neither should the gentleman cause laughter by sarcasm or mockery of the unfortunate. Even in telling jokes, Castiglione warns the courtier to remember 'always our dignity as gentlemen, eschewing vile words and indecorous acts, not contorting the face or person grotesquely.'[27]

---

24 Ibid., II, 144ff.

25 Ibid., I, 64.

26 Ibid., II, 155.

27 Ibid., II, 160.

Castiglione gives a wide representation of types of jokes and various forms of humorous speech. Two of these illustrations involve music. The first involves a peasant boy who makes his first visit to the large city, to Venice to attend the Feast of the Ascension. When the boy returns he is asked what he found most remarkable and he mentioned, among other things, 'so much music and singing that it seemed just like heaven.' When pressed further what kind of music most pleased him, he follows with this description of one who had seen for the first time the slide trumpet. The instrument was played with one hand holding the mouthpiece on the lips, while the other hand made the entire remaining instrument slide back and forth.

> [The music] was all good. But I especially noticed someone playing on a strange sort of trumpet which with every move he thrust down his throat more than two palms' length, and then straight away would draw it out, only to thrust it down again; and you never saw the like![28]

The second illustration involved a play on words. A duke, about to cross a river, gave an order for the appropriate signal to his trumpeter: *Passa* ['Cross now']. The trumpeter turned to the duke and answered very respectfully: *Passi la Signoria Vostra* ['After you!'].[29]

We are given one final view of court entertainment music, when the aristocratic company has tired of their discussions of the desirable qualities of the courtier and are in the mood to dance. At this time, we are told, they call upon Barletta, 'a delightful musician and an excellent dancer, who always kept the Court agreeably entertained.'[30]

---

[28] Ibid., II, 163.

[29] Ibid., II, 170ff.

[30] Ibid., I, 104.

Michelangelo on Art and Music

> *I regret ... that I am dying just as I am beginning*
> *to learn the alphabet of my profession.*[1]
> Michelangelo

FEW PERSONS WOULD OBJECT to our calling Michelangelo (1475–1564) the greatest sculptor who has yet been born. Fortunately for him, painting and sculpture were becoming recognized as arts, as opposed to the 'crafts' they had been since the ancient world. We can see him arguing for this new definition in a conversation he reportedly had with a contemporary.

> Works ought not to be esteemed because of the amount of time employed and lost in the labor, but because of the merit of the knowledge and of the hand which did them; for if it were not so, they would not pay more to a lawyer for an hour's examination of an important case, than to a weaver for as much cloth as he may weave during the course of his whole life.[2]

But this was a view of society which was only in the process of changing. Michelangelo would live long enough to see his efforts recognized as art, but he was born too early to enjoy the financial rewards appropriate to his work.

> Painting and sculpture, hard work and fair dealing have been my ruin and things go continually from bad to worse. It would have been better had I been put to making matches in my youth.[3]

When Michelangelo speaks of hard work, as he did above, it was not just a figure of speech. He mentioned the sheer difficulty of the labor of the sculptor.

> I'm living here in the greatest discomfort and in a state of extreme fatigue; I do nothing but work day and night and have endured and am enduring such fatigue that if I had to do the work over again I do not believe I should survive.[4]

Two similar complaints date from the period of his work on the Sistine Chapel.

> I am living here in a state of great anxiety and of the greatest physical fatigue; I have no friends of any sort and want none. I haven't even time enough to eat as I should.[5]

......

---

[1] Bernini, quoted in M. de Chantelou, *Journal du voyage du Cavalier Bernini* (Paris, 1885), 140.

[2] Quoted in Robert J. Clements, *Michelangelo: A Self-Portrait* (New York: New York University Press, 1968), 15ff.

[3] Letter to Luigi del Riccio, Fall, 1542, in *The Letters of Michelangelo*, trans. E. H. Ramsden (Stanford: Stanford University Press, 1963), II, 26.

[4] Letter to Buonarroto Buonarrota, October 19, 1507, in *The Letters of Michelangelo*, I, 40.

[5] Letter to Buonarroto Buonarrota, October 17, 1509, in Ibid., I, 54.

> I work harder than anyone who has ever lived. I'm not well and worn out with this stupendous labor.[6]

In a rare comment on the end of this labor, he is reported to have expressed the same philosophy as Castiglione's definition of the nonchalance which should characterize the work of the gentleman.

> I wish to tell you, Francisco de Hollanda, of an exceedingly great beauty in this science of ours, of which perhaps you are aware, and which I think you consider the highest, namely, that what one has most to strive for in painting is to do the work with a great amount of labor and study in such a way that it may afterward appear, however much it was labored, to have been done almost quickly and almost without any labor, and very easily, although it was not.[7]

Michelangelo was also a poet with a considerable body of works. Often these poems speak of love and he always addresses this topic with great emotion. One example will suffice:

> How much less pain I'd have from dying quickly,
> Than, one by one, a thousand deaths to suffer
> From her who wills my death because I love her.
> Oh what infinite grief
> My heart feels when it chances to perceive
> That she I love so greatly feels no love.[8]

One of the core thoughts of Michelangelo was that art is not found in the art object, nor in the hands which created it. Usually he spoke of the art being in the mind of the artist, but often there is a divine connection behind it. This was an idea he chose to express through poetry. In a madrigal, he writes,

> As a sure guide to me in my vocation
> The idea of beauty, which is a mirror and a lamp to both my arts,
> Was bestowed upon me at birth.
> Whosoever conceives otherwise is mistaken.[9]

Similarly, in a sonnet.

> If my rough hammer in hard stones can form
> A human semblance, one and then another,
> Set moving by the agent who is holder,
> Watcher and guide, its course is not its own.
>
> But that divine One, staying in Heaven at home,
> Gives others beauty, more to itself, self-mover;

---

[6] Letter to Buonarroto Buonarrota, July 24, 1512, in Ibid., I, 70.

[7] Quoted in Clements, *Michelangelo: A Self-Portrait*, 18.

[8] *Complete Poems of Michelangelo*, trans. Creighton Gilbert (Princeton: Princeton University Press, 1963), 8.

[9] Quoted in Anthony Blunt, *Artistic Theory in Italy, 1450–1600* (Oxford: Clarendon Press, 1959), 69.

> If hammers can't be made without a hammer,
> From that one living all the others come.¹⁰

In the poetry of his later years, an even stronger association with the divine Beauty appears.

> Of Thy mercy, make me see Thee in all places.
> If mortal beauty sets me aflame, my fire shall seem spent when brought near to Thine.
> Yet in Thy flame shall I be once more on fire.¹¹

An early letter in which Michelangelo addresses the distinction between mind and hand is a complaint regarding his treatment at the time he was working on the tomb for Julius II.

> I'll always go on working for Pope Clement with such powers as I have, which are slight, as I'm an old man—with this proviso, that the taunts, to which I see I am being subjected, cease, because they very much upset me and prevented me from doing the work I want to do for several months now. For one cannot work at one thing with the hands and at another with the head, particularly in the case of marble. Here it is said that they are meant to spur me on, but I assure you they are poor spurs which drive one back.¹²

Michelangelo states this principle very clearly in some of his poems, one of which reads,

> The greatest artist has no conception
> Which a single block of marble does not
> Potentially contain within its mass,
> But only a hand obedient to the mind
> Can penetrate to this image.¹³

Nothing testifies to this more clearly than Michelangelo's unfinished sculptures. Anyone who sees one of these pieces is struck by the illusion of a work already finished within the marble, just waiting for the unneeded stone to be struck away.

Perhaps the fact that there is relatively little commentary on his finished pieces in his letters is due to his awareness that the version in his mind was more beautiful than that which he completed. A contemporary, Condivi, who recalls Michelangelo having discussed this very point with him, described him as having had,

> a most powerful imagination, whence it comes, chiefly, that he is little contented with his works and has always underrated them, his hand not appearing to carry out the ideas he has conceived in his mind.¹⁴

---

10 *Complete Poems of Michelangelo*, 28.

11 Quoted in Blunt, *Artistic Theory in Italy*, 79.

12 Letter to Giovan Francesco Fattucci, October 24, 1525, in *The Letters of Michelangelo*, I, 162.

13 Quoted in Blunt, *Artistic Theory in Italy*, 73.

14 Quoted in Ibid., 72.

In this regard, it is interesting that Michelangelo criticized Raphael for not finding his art within, but 'only acquiring it by long study.'[15]

Art being defined as within the artist, it is no surprise to find Michelangelo equating a man's character with his art. In a comment recalled by his contemporary, de Hollanda, he speaks of the painting of religious art, which, of course, he was much involved in his career.

> In order to imitate in some degree the venerable image of Our Lord, it is not enough to be a painter, a great and skillful master; I believe that one must further be of blameless life, even if possible a saint, that the Holy Spirit may inspire one's understanding.[16]

In this regard, Michelangelo praised the artist Fra Angelico, but was very modest regarding his own character.

> This good man painted with his heart, so that he was able with his pencil to give outward expression to his inner devotion and piety, which I can never achieve, since I do not feel myself to have so well disposed a heart.[17]

Regarding the purpose of art, in a letter written to Niccolo Franco we find a definition which seems very much in the spirit of Aristotle's famous concept of catharsis.

> And who does not know that a noble and sublime subject gives greatness to our souls and lends wings to the most humble and modest intellect?[18]

One of the most familiar topics relative to the aesthetics of art is the question regarding whether art should imitate nature. It is a topic Michelangelo addresses several times, for it appears to have been for him most natural to imitate the beauty of nature. A contemporary has reported him saying,

> The painting which I so much vaunt and praise will be the imitation of some single thing among those which immortal God made with great care and knowledge and which He invented and painted, like a Master: and so downward, whether animals or birds, dispensing perfection according as each merits it. And in my judgment that is the excellent and divine painting which is most like and best imitates any work of immortal God, whether a human figure, or a wild and strange animal, or a simple and easy fish, or a bird in the air, or any other creature.[19]

It follows, that Michelangelo's method, according to Condivi, was first one of observation and choice.

---

[15] Condivi, quoted in Blunt, *Artistic Theory in Italy*, 76.

[16] Quoted in Blunt, *Artistic Theory in Italy*, 71.

[17] Quoted in Ibid., 78.

[18] Quoted in Clements, *Michelangelo: A Self-Portrait*, 13.

[19] Quoted in Ibid., 12.

> He loved not only human beauty but universally every beautiful thing … choosing the beauty in nature, as the bees gather honey from the flowers using it afterwards in their works.[20]

One contemporary recalls an amusing reflection on this subject, made when Michelangelo was lecturing his students against haste.

> Whereas Art, which is imitative of Nature (if it wishes to be praised for its function) should not depart from that very method which Nature uses in the generation of animals: the longer the life that these animals are to have, the more time Nature spends in producing them.[21]

But what if someone questioned whether Michelangelo, or any artist, could really equal Nature? Niccolo Martelli recalled Michelangelo's answer when the complaint was made that his portrait of Lorenzo and Giuliano de' Medici was not 'life-like.' Well, said Michelangelo,

> A thousand years from now no one could judge that they looked otherwise![22]

When discussing his own paintings, Michelangelo, clearly aware that he was an even greater sculptor, often denied that he was a painter to begin with. Toward the beginning of his work on the Sistine Chapel, he wrote his father expressing his dissatisfaction with the progress of the work, adding,

> This is due to the difficulty of the work and also because it is not my profession.[23]

When the work was completed Michelangelo signed a receipt, on May 10, 1508, in which his careful choice of words speaks for itself.

> I, Michelangelo Buonarroti, *sculptor*, have received from his Holiness 500 ducats of the Camara, on account, for the *paintings* of the vault of the Chapel of Pope Sixtus.[24]

Being both a painter and a sculptor, Michelangelo appears to have given considerable thought to the aesthetic differences between these two arts. He once offered to a contemporary this distinction:

> This must be kept in mind, that the closer you see paintings approach good sculpture, the better they will be; and the more sculptures will approach paintings, the worse you will hold them to be.[25]

---

[20] Quoted in Blunt, *Artistic Theory in Italy*, 62.
[21] Giraldi Cinzio, *Hecatommithi, overo Cento novelle* (Venice, 1608), II, 218.
[22] Quoted in Charles De Tolnay, *The Medici Chapel* (Princeton, 1948), 68.
[23] Letter to Lodovico Buonarrota, January 27, 1509, in *The Letters of Michelangelo*, I, 48.
[24] Quoted in Clements, *Michelangelo: A Self-Portrait*, 19.
[25] Giovan Battista Armenini, *De' veri precetti della pittura* (Ravenna, 1586), 226ff.

He elaborated on the meaning of this in a letter to Benedetto Varchi in 1547 and then explains that he had now come to understand painting and sculpture to be two forms of the same purpose in art.

> I admit that it seems to me that painting may be held to be good in the degree in which it approximates to relief, and relief to be bad in the degree in which it approximates to painting. I used therefore to think that painting derived its light from sculpture and that between the two the difference was as that between the sun and the moon.
>
> Now, since I have read the passage in your paper where you say that, philosophically speaking, things which have the same end are one and the same, I have altered my opinion and maintain that, if in face of greater difficulties, impediments and labors, greater judgment does not make for greater nobility, then painting and sculpture are one and the same, and being held to be so, no painter ought to think less of sculpture than of painting, and similarly no sculptor less of painting than of sculpture. By sculpture I mean that which is fashioned by the effort of cutting away, that which is fashioned by the method of building up being like unto painting. It suffices that as both, that is to say sculpture and painting, proceed from one and the same faculty of understanding, we may bring them to amicable terms and desist from such disputes, because they take up more time than the execution of the figures themselves. If he who wrote that painting is nobler than sculpture understood as little about the other things of which he writes—my maidservant could have expressed them better.[26]

An occasional remark by Michelangelo, however, reveals that his true love was sculpture. A contemporary reports his having observed,

> There is as much difference between painting and sculpture as between shadow and truth.[27]

And we are especially fond of a remark reported by French visitor:

> If a room were adorned with tapestries woven with gold, and in another room there were only one beautiful statue, the latter room would appear to be adorned royally and would make the first look like a nun's cell.[28]

Michelangelo made one very interesting observation regarding architecture. It is a reflection we wish he had chosen to discuss at length.

> It is therefore indisputable that the limbs of architecture are derived from the limbs of man. No one who has not been or is not a good master of the human figure, particularly of anatomy, can comprehend this.[29]

Michelangelo seemed to share with a great many early philosophers a general distrust for the broad public and its ability to understand and judge art. A contemporary reports him having said,

---

[26] Letter to Benedetto Varchi, March, 1547, in *The Letters of Michelangelo*, II, 75.

[27] Anton Francesco Doni, *Disegno* (Venice, 1549), 44.

[28] Quoted in Chantelou, *Journal du voyage du Cavalier Bernini*, 103.

[29] Letter to Cardinal ..., December, 1550, in *The Letters of Michelangelo*, II, 129.

> How wrong are those simpletons of whom the world is full, who look more at a green, a red, or similar high color than at the figures which show spirit and movement.[30]

It is to be regretted that Michelangelo so rarely mentioned music. The reader will recall that Leonardo da Vinci was particularly jealous that music was a respected member of the Liberal Arts, while painting was not. Since Michelangelo never once mentions having heard an actual performance of art music, it is possible that he also felt some jealousy toward the popularity of the now great art music of the High Renaissance.

On one occasion, he sent some poetry he had composed to Fra Sebastiano del Piombo in Rome to have them set to music as madrigals. They were set to music by Constanzo Festa and Giacomo Concilion and after they were returned, Michelangelo wrote a note of thanks, pretending not to have even heard the music himself.

> I have received the two madrigals and Ser Giovan Francesco has had them performed several times; according to what he tells me, they are considered wonderful things to sing; the words didn't merit such a setting ... Please will you let me know what I should do for the master who wrote the music, so that I may not appear more ignorant and ungrateful than need be.[31]

However, one passing remark to de Hollanda, in the course of criticizing the painting of Flanders, offers a clue that he may have been a more experienced listener after all.

> It will please likewise friars and nuns, and also some noble persons who have no ear for true harmony.[32]

Surely when visiting his home in Florence, Michelangelo must have heard fine performances of great music, performances characterized by the work of passionate musicians. One finds a hint of such experience in a poem where he describes the music of a goatherd he heard while engaging in one of his occasional walks into the country. He may not have found the music sophisticated, but he did notice its communication of feeling as the peasant was 'pouring his soul out.'

> It is a novel and superior pleasure
> To see the daring goats climbing a rock,
> Making one peak and then the next their pasture,
> And down below their owner, with harsh music,
> Pouring his soul out in a rough-hewn measure,
> Playing as he stands, or at a gentle walk.[33]

---

[30] Armenini, *De' veri precetti della pittura*, 72.

[31] Letter to Fra Sebastiano del Piombo, August, 1533, in *The Letters of Michelangelo*, I, 185. He mentions another madrigal, apparently set to his poetry, in a letter to Luigi del Ricco, in the Summer of 1542 [*The Letters of Michelangelo*, II, 17.]

[32] Quoted in Clements, *Michelangelo: A Self-Portrait*, 37.

[33] *Complete Poems of Michelangelo*, 42.

Girolamo Cardano on Music

> Nature has made me capable, pious, faithful, meditative, inventive, courageous, cunning, crafty, sarcastic, industrious, diligent, ingenious, impertinent, contemptuous of religion, grudging, envious, sad, treacherous, magician and sorcerer, miserable, hateful, lascivious, solitary, disagreeable, rude, divinator, changeable, irresolute, indecent, quarrelsome, and because of the conflicts between my nature and soul I am not understood even by those with whom I associate most frequently.[1]
>
> Cardano

GIROLAMO CARDANO (1501–1576) was certainly one of the most interesting intellectuals of the sixteenth century. He stands apart from other authors on music for many of his views characterize music in a negative light. We have seen nothing quite like these views since the earliest years of the Christian era.

Cardano's education began under his father, a lawyer in Milan, who taught him arithmetic, geometry[2] and astrology. Music lessons were made possible, secretly, through the aid of his mother. In later years he would remember this music teacher, Leo Oglonus, for his high moral standards. As for himself, in his autobiography Cardano recalled 'wandering through Milan from dusk until daybreak, dripping with perspiration from the exertion of serenading with his musical instruments.'[3] A friend, who later became the Archbishop of Milan, recalled that Cardano performed with grace.[4]

After a violent family argument, the father allowed Cardano to study medicine at the University of Pavia, but after one year the university was closed due to war and he transferred to the University of Padua. Here he proved an outstanding student, was active in debate and obtained the student office of Rector. He received the Doctor of Medicine degree, after three faculty ballots, but was refused permission, due to the suspicion that he was of illegitimate birth, by the College of Physicians in Milan, to practice in the town where his mother now lived.

Cardano settled in the village of Sacco, near Padua, where he experienced little financial success in his medical practice, but otherwise enjoyed his most pleasant years.

---

[1] Quoted in Oystein Ore, *Cardano The Gambling Scholar* (New York: Dover, 1953), 25ff.
[2] The father was consulted several times on geometry by Leonardo da Vinci.
[3] *Hieronymi Cardani Mediolensis opera omnia*, I, 1.
[4] Alan Wykes, *Doctor Cardano* (London, 1969), 18.

> I gambled, played musical instruments, took walks, and was of good cheer and studied only rarely. I had no pains, no fears; I was treated with esteem and respect and I associated with the nobles of Venice. In short, it was the springtime of my life.[5]

After his marriage, Cardano moved to Milan, where his repeated requests for permission to practice medicine were turned down. He was able to gain appointment as a lecturer in mathematics for the Piatti foundation, which was the turning point in his career. He attracted large audiences for his lectures and published his first two books on mathematics in 1539.

With this boost to his self-confidence, Cardano began to fight back against the doctors of Milan. He published a book called *On the Bad Practices of Medicine* which was immediately popular with the public.

> The things which give most reputation to a physician nowadays are his manners, servants, carriage, clothes, smartness, and caginess, all displayed in a sort of artificial and insipid way; learning and experience seem to count for nothing.[6]

Public pressure caused the College of Physicians to relent and within a few years Cardano became one of the most famous physicians in Europe. Receiving offers from nobles everywhere for his services, Cardano traveled widely and was always received with the greatest acclaim.

Cardano took advantage of his fame by beginning to publish an incredible stream of books on nearly every subject, including mathematics, astronomy, physics, morals, dialectics, ethics, philosophy, the immortality of the soul, the mysteries of eternity, works of history, music, games of chance, chess, gems, dreams, and religious studies. His *De Subtilitate Rerum*, a work on science and natural philosophy became one of the best sellers during the second half of the sixteenth century. Another popular book, *Consolation*, was translated into English in 1573, read by Shakespeare and is considered to have influenced Hamlet's famous soliloquy. In all there were 131 published works, 111 in manuscript and another 170 which he burned, considering them worthless. It seems clear that this enormous output was driven by a passion to perpetuate his name, something he became obsessed with during his youth after noticing that a close family friend was never mentioned again after his death.

Cardano's spirit was completely broken in 1560 when his son, Giambatista, was imprisoned for the poisoning of his unfaithful wife. In spite of the efforts of Cardano, Giambatista was hanged at age twenty-six, after having his left hand struck off under torture. Another son, Aldo, saddened his father by being repeatedly jailed for theft. Cardano resigned his professorship in Milan, but after two years, through the intervention of old friends, accepted a professorship in medicine at the University of Bologna.

---

[5] Quoted in Ore, *Cardano the Gambling Scholar*, 10.

[6] Ibid., 12.

In October 1570 Cardano was arrested as a heretic and placed in jail. He was removed from his university position and forbidden to have any more books published. He moved to Rome where, in spite of his sentence, he was invited to become a member of the College of Physicians and received a pension from the pope.

It is no longer possible to determine why the charge of heresy was brought against him. The most likely reason was a passage in his *De Subtilitate* in which he describes a religious debate between a Christian, Jew, Mohammedan and a heathen, in which he unfortunately forgot to find in favor of the Christian. Otherwise there was nothing in his personal conduct typical of the heretic. In fact, when the King of Denmark wanted him as his personal physician, Cardano answered by writing that it would be repugnant to him to live in a country of heretics (Protestants).

Cardano had few friends and history has never known quite what to think about him. It would be easy to discount much of his writings, for some are filled with contradictions and some are on pseudo-science, such as metoposcopy (determining character by the face), chiromancy (palmistry) and geomancy (predicting the future). Yet, he made significant contributions, such as his description of typhus fever and his discoveries in algebra, including his perception that quadratic equations might have negative roots.

He was best summarized by the famous German mathematician and philosopher Leibniz, who wrote,

> Cardano was a great man with all his faults; without them he would have been incomparable.

Cardano was first and foremost a mathematician and it is in this field that he is most remembered today. It is no surprise, therefore, that in his own catalog of his manuscripts, his music treatise is found listed under the category of mathematics. It was no doubt mathematics he was thinking of when he defined music as 'a discipline which teaches men to recognize the meaning of sounds and to listen to their differences.'[7]

One of the curious aesthetic realities of earlier centuries was that while the third was considered consonant, the sixth was not. With Cardano at times the feeling side of him took precedence over the mathematical side, as, for example, when he asks regarding sixths, 'why should we reject what the ear already approves,' even if the mathematical ratios do not agree. Such things, he concludes, cannot yet be explained.

> So it is necessary to consider why a connection of tones which is pleasing to the ears does not have a rational explanation. Accordingly, the usefulness of the aural sense is clear, but its rationale is found in the discovery of many things which are not yet fully known through experience, or in the need for a proper measure of its use.[8]

---

7 Quoted in Clement Miller, *Hieronymus Cardanus, Writings on Music* ([Rome]: American Institute of Musicology, 1973), 37.

8 Ibid., 104.

It is also interesting that his predilection for mathematics did not lead him to a preference to the polyphonic style, a fact he mentions several times. His preference for the music of his own humanistic generation can be seen in a comment he made after discussing Ockeghem.

> But the music of our day is as much more elegant as it was more elaborate in earlier times.[9]

In the most general sense, Cardano finds the purpose of music in three broad categories.

> There are three reasons for the invention of music, which are pleasure, grief and divine inspiration.[10]

He begins his treatise, *On Music*, with his contention that the real purpose of music must be found in the present, and not in the past.

> I do not consider that music should be esteemed for its antiquity or its glorious inventors, two reasons commonly given in laudatory introductions to the arts, but for its usefulness, excellence, subtlety, and value among other arts and disciplines.[11]

The specific purpose of music which Cardano mentions most frequently is that it is for the purpose of pleasure. He often mentions this by way of defining something, as for example in discussing complex proportions he dismisses the ones resulting in the fastest notes, saying 'whatever the ear cannot perceive does not produce pleasure.'[12] He discusses pleasure with respect to purpose of the various elements of music, as we can see in these reflections on ancient music.

> Harmonic music consisted of words and music and their concord. It was entirely directed towards pleasure. Rhythmic music existed in a similar way in different countries. It is common, popular, and in use now in Africa and Italy, formerly in Judea. It exists to produce a certain pleasure in the minds of the common people. Metric music, which includes artistic poetry, offers much pleasure in epics and fine poetry, and shows the mores of humanity.[13]

In another place, Cardano elaborates on the manner in which emotional content produces pleasure.

> The first rule of artistic music: there is nothing more efficacious for pleasure than proper imitation. It has three parts: manner [*modus*], sense [*sensus*], and sound [*sonus*]. These three do not always coincide. For example, if one imitates the song of small birds, it is not necessary to imitate the sense, for their chirping has no meaning, but only their sound and manner …
>
> We imitate by sense when there is great emotion, such as in the four moods of sorrow, joy, tranquility, and excitement …

---

9   Ibid., 153. Cardano refers here to an unknown 36-voice canon by Ockeghem.
10 Ibid., 175.
11 Ibid., 37.
12 Ibid., 71.
13 Ibid., 96.

> A mood of commiseration proceeds in music in slow and serious notes by dropping downward suddenly from a high range. This imitates the manner of those who weep, for at first they wail in a very high and clear voice and then they end by dropping into a very low and rather muffled groan.[14]

Cardano's most specific reference to music having the purpose of offering solace, and it is one he qualifies, is found in a discussion of the cithara.

> If there is an instrument appropriate to tranquility and also a relation of meter and poetry to it, the instrument will be a cithara and the song will be mournful and almost tragic. In this way we can lighten the cares that result from the misery of human misfortune, although I do not necessarily recommend this.[15]

As an amateur performer himself, it is no surprise that Cardano recommends music for a profitable use of leisure time. In his *The Book on Games of Chance*, in arguing against gambling as a form of leisure, he includes music as one of several more profitable activities, together with his reasons.

> As for the excuse made by some that [gambling] relieves boredom, this would be better done by pleasant reading, or by narrating tales or stories, or by one of the beautiful but not laborious arts. Among the latter, playing the lute or the cembalo, or singing, or composing poetry will be more useful, and for three reasons. First, because such a change from serious business is more praiseworthy than gambling, either since something is produced, as in the case of painting, or because it is according to nature, as in music, or because the man learns something, as in reading ... Second, it does not rob us, against our will, of more time than it should ... Third, such employment of leisure is more respectable and does not present a bad example, as gambling does, particularly to one's children and servants.[16]

In several places Cardano stresses the utilitarian purposes of music. In the following passage, which again mentions its use for leisure, he is concerned primarily with music's contribution to education. Also interesting here is a reference to Aristotle's concept of catharsis, the 'cleansing of the spirit.' Finally, we find here the negative attitude which often enters Cardano's discussion of music, in this case his suggestion that some believe music adversely affects character and in his expression that music affords an 'innocuous' pleasure.

> [Music's] usefulness is divided into three parts, for it pertains to instruction and study, or to the cleansing of the spirit, or to spending time pleasurably in leisure, tranquility, and freedom from the pressure of more serious matters. It is often said that emotions in music reflect weakened and enervated morals, but I believe such emotions consist of gentle virtues, and correspond to those more appropriate to action and also to those most divine virtues suitable for intellectual endeavor. Accordingly music celebrates those moral virtues which are especially appropriate to that useful quality which pertains to learning. Teachers and disciplinarians have agreed on the expiative and purgative

---

14 Ibid., 142ff.

15 Ibid., 204.

16 Sidney Henry Gould, *Cardano, The Gambling Scholar* (Princeton: Princeton University Press, 1953), 186. Cardano also makes the interesting observation that the Christians tolerate gambling, but do not allow cursing.

force of strong emotions. When these emotions subside they may become excessively reversed and softened by giving way especially to emotions of misery and pity, causing dejection and depression. Music also proposes to fill such moods with a certain innocuous pleasure.[17]

In a discussion entitled 'On the Value of Music,' Cardano's negative attitudes about music become pronounced. Music may be honorable, but it is not essential or necessary. We see here one of his more heated attacks on singers and how having them in his home, he claims, corrupted his own children. It is better, he concludes to have the children play instruments that do not require any other musician—although not the wind instruments, for reasons of health.

> It is useful to consider whether the study of music is worthwhile. It appears to have value, for both Plato and Aristotle state that boys should be instructed in it. Reason also recommends this, since one cannot be constantly engaged in laborious pursuits, so that leisure time is a necessity. Yet leisure that is inane and empty cannot create a rewarding life, because a rewarding life consists in work. Thus it is necessary to engage in some sort of activity during leisure hours; even though it is not necessary or essential it should be honest and honorable. Such an activity is the study of music.
>
> Music is also of worth because it is a pleasing pastime and is useful for discipline and as a cultural value of life. Also, since it affords pleasure without detriment it is beneficial to all and especially to children.
>
> Yet if one considers our presently complicated way of singing [polyphony], which consists of many persons singing together and which cannot take place at one's own leisure, since there is a need for fellow singers and since so many of them have dissolute morals, we conclude that this practice is really of no use to anyone. You find hardly any musician in our time who does not abound in every kind of vice, and thus such a musician is the greatest impediment not only to a poor and busy man but to all men in general. And why don't you find a musician among the distinguished men of our time, men such as Erasmus, Alciatus, Bude, Jason, Vesalius, and Gesner?
>
> But since this kind of music has subverted my own home, so to speak, I will present the facts in my own case. For not only did I sustain a heavy loss of money, but what is worse, I corrupted the morals of my own children. It is hard to assemble four or five person who can sing readily. Since we want this activity to take place frequently it occurs during leisure time. If we do it at home the singers will be maintained at great expense and they will corrupt the characters of our young boys and adolescents, for most of them are drunkards and gluttons, also wanton, fickle, impatient, coarse, indolent, and tainted with every kind of unlawful desire. The best of them are fools.
>
> Does this mean then that music must be expelled from the home and the education of children? Not at all. Music has three attributes: sound, rhythm, and cognition arising from perception. Cognition is useful in all activities, in recognizing men of talent, in deriving pleasure from listening to singers, and in pursuing music yourself, although I will say later how you do this. It is also worthwhile to grasp the rhythm for the sake of the poetry and for the pleasure, understanding, and practice of the music. But sound must be employed to the degree that it can be applied to musical instruments, not to singing polyphonically. Such instruments are the lute, lira, pipe organ, and other string instruments. These instruments are complete in themselves and need only one person to play them, so that one can practice by himself and receive pleasure. In this kind of music one can satisfy the three conditions that Aristotle proposed, namely, the confirmation or change of morals, moods, or actions. These conditions also apply to the present times, both in the morals of children and adolescents and in the organization of life.

---

[17] Miller, *Hieronymus Cardanus, Writings on Music*, 105.

> Yet the rich can learn polyphonic music thoroughly and can form a group of singers from chosen men; although this is difficult it still can be done. But for the poor, or children, or youths, or those who want to teach their children at home, social music is not practical. Understanding it is more beneficial than participation, also having a knowledge of the complete instruments, but not of the kind of instrument in which the cheeks are puffed up; among such instruments I detest mostly the playing of horns, because their use is neither distinguished nor noble nor beneficial to the brain, lungs, or abdomen, for it causes hernias. And when Aristotle did not approve of the use of the same instruments that we have just praised, he was considering their public use, while we were thinking of their appropriateness for individuals.[18]

Later he continues in the same vein, denigrating singers and now even finding complaints with playing a solo instrument.

> In our time a person may seek to study music, and when he has barely mastered it after much effort he finds that there is a lack of fellow singers. And even if he meets with them they often make mistakes, causing laughter among the listeners, so that he gets contempt in place of praise and sorrow in place of pleasure. When they do sing well one wants to be more prominent than another, a circumstance which creates tension.
>
> If the instruction has been satisfactory another concern may come to mind, [should] you learn to play the lute or recorder. How much labor and tedium is there in this effort? After an entire year of work, if the study is as successful as you had wished, you will be pleased with a few things, but not without great effort. Meanwhile one thing or other will be lacking, and even if everything has turned out well you find that your efforts are disdained more than they are praised. Your incentive disappears, and cares of the family and business interfere. One becomes a servant of fellow musicians, and must put up with all their faults and troublesome natures.
>
> So you can see how hostile these things are to tranquility; nor is the source of this impediment to be found anywhere but in ourselves. But you say: 'I enjoy music a great deal and have studied since childhood.' In that case there is no instrument more perfect than a lira, none more unlimited, none more pleasant, none more comfortable. Yet it causes a great deal of inconvenience when strings are tightened, loosened, changed or restrung. When they are tuned they break from humidity and rain or from dryness and wind.[19]

Cardano calls the first elements of music, tone, pitch and volume. Then in an example of the contradictions which abound in his writings, he says the quality of a tone *differs* with either of these two, although he immediately defines quality in these same terms.

> There are harsh [*asperae*] tones that may be high, or powerful, or weak, although in a weak tone harshness is less offensive. In the same way there are soft or mild tones that may be high or low or powerful or weak.[20]

---

[18] Ibid., 197ff. Aristotle disapproved of the aulos in education, but only because it was too exciting.
[19] Ibid., 200.
[20] Ibid., 39.

It is interesting that Cardano associates time in music with emotions.

> There is nothing that moves the affections more than the division of temporal values.[21]

Regarding consonance and dissonance, Cardano believed that the ear does not recognize either consonance or dissonance in 'intervals that are widely separated.'[22] In several places he suggests that the ear accepts dissonance only when heard in passing.

> Dissonances are not allowed to remain sounding, for just as with men who have become frozen stiff through immoderate cold and remain so even when heat is applied, so also a consonance following a dissonance will greatly please the ears if the dissonance's movement is not delayed, but if the dissonance is retained it will destroy all harmony.[23]

Cardano also becomes contradictory when discussing the ancient modes. In one place he describes Dorian as 'sharp, unpolished, hard,' in another context as 'filled with majesty' and in yet another place that it 'withdrew from passionate emotions and led to moderation.'[24]

Cardano also discusses the physical nature of instruments at length, including the materials used in their construction ('The best gut strings come from dogs'). Some of his observations make little sense, as when he distinguishes between a *fistula* in which the 'tone is formed in the throat' and the recorder or *syrinx*, 'which merely uses the breath but forms the tone within itself.'[25]

His most interesting discussion on this topic provides several criteria for judging the excellence of musical instruments,[26] most of which are aesthetic in nature.

1. The range should be ample, at least two octaves.
2. The sound should be pleasing, not harsh or clamorous.
3. The sound should be easy to produce. For these three reasons trumpets are imperfect and inferior: they are far more difficult to blow than recorders, their tone is raucous and clamorous, and they exceed an octave range by only one tone. Horns [*cornua*] are also more inferior because of the last two reasons.
4. They should sound well with the human voice and other instruments. On this account recorders are the least praiseworthy, for hardly any other instrument blends less well with the voice and other instruments.
5. Those with many strings are preferable to those with three or less.
6. They should be able to sustain a tone.
7. They should have a full tone.

---

[21] Ibid., 137.

[22] Ibid., 40.

[23] Ibid., 42.

[24] Ibid., 97, 100, 101.

[25] Ibid., 51. In Ibid., 60, Cardano discusses the nature of breath used in a wind instrument, but he is generally misinformed.

[26] Ibid., 55.

8. They should be capable of producing very small and a great number of intervals. In this regard the lute is superior to the organ.

Cardano also ranks the aesthetic order of instruments according to their similarity to the human voice. Thus winds are superior to strings, although he hastens to say that the viol is preferable to the fife.[27] We learn the full extent of his meaning of 'similarity' in this remarkable description of the possibilities of the recorder.

> The things that are true for the recorder are true for all instruments, but they are even more appropriate for this instrument. A particular property is imitation of the human voice, not simple imitation (for this is common to all instruments) but rather exact imitation is proper to the instrument. This happens by using a relaxed tone in laments, a strong tone in excitement, a smooth, connected tone in serious moods, and so forth concerning the other emotions.[28]

Most interesting is this passage which reveals that bagpipe and string players sometimes simultaneously played and sang!

> It is common to all pipers and to string players who sing as they play that they should not move their heads about nor contort their lips nor do anything indecorous. Again, they should always adjust their voices and sound by listening, and should carefully watch others beating time. Thirdly, they should keep the beat, which is far easier to do in singing than in playing, since a constant pulse is less evident. Finally, in instruments which are played by blowing a pleasing quality must be kept in every respect, for although in singing one can pronounce words, in playing tonal sweetness and a suitable imitation of mood reach the highest summit of artistry.[29]

Finally, Cardano mentions the actions of wind players necessary in accommodating the several tuning systems currently in use.

> Just as musicians of our time have given sufficient attention to the chromatic genus ... so in the enharmonic they have been negligent because they have not understood it up to the present, although many woodwind and horn players apply it by gradually raising and lowering tones, as in dividing the distance between *mi* and *fa* so that the last tone forms a concord.[30]

In the following description of the basic requirements for a good singer, we find the final line most interesting—that a man is called a musician on the basis of his ears, that is, in his success in actual performance. This is a very significant departure from the long tradition of medieval writers, who always made a careful distinction between singers and musicians, by which they meant that the knowledge of the mathematics behind music distinguishes the musician—and therefore singers were not musicians.

---

[27] Ibid.

[28] Ibid., 69.

[29] Ibid., 189.

[30] Ibid., 127.

> It happens that an innately vocal sound acquires most of its attributes or its impediments from nature. Indeed, if a voice is to be pleasant it should be pure, sonorous, firm, and capable of rising high and descending low. Also, it should have a youthful quality and should be capable of producing natural differences in whole tones and semitones. Finally, the singer should have an adaptable and highly developed sense of hearing, for the ears are more influential than the voice. They direct not only one's own musical sounds but also those of others as well as those of instruments. A man deserves to be called a musician because of his ears, not his voice.[31]

Cardano follows this with curious reflections on vocal technique and its effect on character.

> It is proper to sing motionlessly and with an open mouth, yet not indecorously, so that the sound is not checked by the lips or by the teeth. A low tone arises from the chest and a high tone from the head, that is, it is expelled from the palate, although its origin is the larynx. This is the reason why those who practice music assiduously from childhood on, injure themselves from constant singing and become mentally dull and morally deficient.

In another place, Cardano presents a major discussion of, and a particularly hostile attack on, singers under the title, 'Precepts for Singers.' Perhaps the most interesting subjects which Cardano mentions here are the ill health effects of singing, his belief that it is the words, and not the music itself, which convey emotion and the reference to improvisation in polyphonic music.

> The first precept pertains to morals. Singers are accused of three things (and not without cause):
> 1. Their morals are depraved, they are gluttons and disreputable purveyors of every kind of vice. During their leisure time they constantly associate with those who live in debauchery and themselves acquire depraved morals …
> 2. They are accused of acting like fools; also, few have money, for riches follow the prudent. Their foolishness results above all from intemperance, especially drinking wine, and also because their musical tones are carried to the brain with force and weaken it. They associate with the imprudent and occupy themselves with fun and frolics. They also teach, but their pedagogy is senseless …
>
> The second precept is that:
> 1. a singer should know how to produce notes very correctly and very swiftly.
> 2. He should have a steady beat and keep it absolutely even …
> 3. His eyes should always look ahead, so that if any difficult place occurs he will be prepared for it.
> 4. He should examine the music before beginning …
> 5. Let him take the greatest care to sing exactly on pitch and not let the note rise or drop …
> 6. Let him produce a tone that is clear but not violent, for in this way many singers suffer a ruptured blood vessel or a hernia.
> 7. A singer produces a pleasant tone gradually, for from a hard and violent breath … a harsh tone will result.

---

[31] Ibid., 107.

The third precept states that you must pass from the notes to the words, and this should be observed carefully, for music is ridiculous which is sung only on *ut*, *re*, *me*, *fa*, *sol*, *la*. There are four reasons for this:

1. What is heard should always be the same as what you have seen;
2. In this way you can truly convey the music's meaning, which depends mostly on the words, whether grave, doleful, or vivacious;
3. When one person sings *re*, another *sol*, and another *fa*, this ... causes great confusion in the music [a reference to polyphonic music];
4. Thus the music is not complete in your ears, and its consonances are understood only by naming the notes but not by their harmony.

The fourth precept states that after you have learned the words you may relinquish the beat gradually, for in this way you compel your ears to listen to the other parts ... If you lose your place you will immediately find it again as you listen to the other singers ... The beat must be retained privately with the first finger and not by the ear alone ... This is especially helpful in regard to what I said about the lack of time beating in woodwind and lira players, since they cannot perform this hand action and are so busy playing.

The fifth precept ... is that first the songs of others should be studied, not of all composers but of those who are especially known for skill and beauty ...

The sixth precept depends on the preceding one. It is in two parts, as it can be accomplished by the ear and by the voice. For you will learn to sing [improvisation] above another voice-part which moves in breves so as to regulate the second apart ... Next you will sing against two, three, or more parts.

The seventh precept [is that] you shall train your ears so carefully that you can recognize the movements of individual voices and their harmonic content ... [The singer] should be careful not to correct someone else needlessly, which is a fault of a great many singers as they show off in front of the listeners.[32]

For Cardano, song meant poetry. It is in this context that he says, 'song is related to music.'

> A song is related to music just as it relates to sound. But since it pertains largely to poetry it reaches the highest perfection in their combination.[33]

Cardano provides a lengthy discussion on the principles of composition for music with words. The focus here again is on his belief that it is the words, and not the music, which conveys meaning. It is for this reason that he stresses the ethical character of the words and the importance of the maintenance of their mood. His statement that the listener cannot recognize a fugal passage unless the same words are maintained, reveals the extent to which the sixteenth-century listener focused on the text in preference to the music.

> Care should be taken that words set to music are serious and honorable. To be avoided are obscene, base, vile, filthy, vulgar, and bacchanalian texts ... From such a song a listener will get not so much pleasure as he will be offended by the subject matter of the poem or the vileness of the text, and a musician who writes notes above such a text is himself made disreputable. The mind is revolted by

---

32 Ibid., 182ff.
33 Ibid., 108.

such a base and uncouth kind of song in which nothing worthy of the art can be created. Artistic forms to be used are heroic, lyric, and decently amatory poems, also elegies, commemorations of saints, laments, prayers and many others which avoid all foulness, wantonness, and turpitude.

Moods should be applied to subject matter and text. There are four simple and rather celebrated groupings: humility and pride, excitement and calm, joy and sorrow, and cruelty and tenderness. From the last two groups comes alacrity, namely, from joy and cruelty, and weeping from tenderness and sadness, for a song that is sad and full of compassion is appropriate to excite weeping. In addition there are other individual types, as prudence and boldness, amorousness and lowliness, virtue and wantonness, seriousness and frivolity, and many others, but these are well known and effective. In each type there are three intermediaries, for either they have no part in either extreme, or they are mixed and participate in both, or they are varied and are not consistent.

A song should always retain its mood, but within a mood's limits it can wander freely; in this way it will not appear disordered nor will its variety bring a satiety of different styles.

Care must be taken that a song does not sound too empty because many voices are silent longer than they are heard. The opposite must be avoided, in which the voices are like racers running continually on a track from beginning to end, for the listeners will feel no pleasure and the singers will get no rest.

Care must also be taken that a song is not so very short that the end is reached while the listeners are still hoping to hear the fullness of the harmony, or so long that the song produces weariness for the listeners and labor for the singers.

When a song contains a *fuga* or exact imitation the same words must be repeated, otherwise the artistry of the music will be lost, for the musical imitation will hardly be recognized with a change of words.

All doleful songs and those evoking compassion should be weighty and stable. All lively songs require notes of short time value … A rousing kind of song is written when syllables are sung very quickly and on the same pitch. We use this type in battle music, for such songs are especially lively.

A song should not begin with dissonant tones, and they also should not strike together, for this is troublesome to singers and detrimental to art.[34]

Regarding the dance, Cardano observes, 'In antiquity dancing was called a sixth part of music.'[35] By this the Greek's meant that dance was a form of music you could see. This viewpoint must be understood in their constant reference to the fact that music is the only art which one cannot see. A more interesting observation on the relationship of ancient dance and music, and one we have not found in extant ancient literature, is that the movements of Greek choral performances were patterned on even earlier statues.

> Dancing and gesticulation express the ample movements that were left from antique statues, and the movements were then transferred from the figures to choral dances, and from choral dances to wrestling schools.[36]

---

34 Ibid., 149ff.

35 Ibid., 117.

36 Ibid., 119.

Finally, Cardano presents a section called 'Musical Problems,' in which he poses rhetorical questions, much like the famous *Problems* of Aristotle. In the third question quoted here, we again see Cardano with a negative perspective of music.

> Why does one tone tend to induce sleep while harmony and aural pleasure consist of many concordant tones? Is it because sleep does not overcome us because of pleasure but rather because of weariness?
>
> ......
>
> Why does a musical proportion consist of unequal and dissimilar numbers while arithmetic and geometric proportions arise from similar numbers? ... Is it because the highest pleasure in human affairs cannot exist without a corresponding pain?
>
> ......
>
> Why do musicians rarely become rich? We exempt those who serve under kings, for 'to have pleased rulers is not the final reward.' Is it because the art is esteemed lightly and is not a necessity of life, so that it is considered servile and unworthy of large gifts? Or is it because its practitioners, addicted to sensual pleasure and gluttony, squander money as fast as they make it? Or is it because the art loses favor on account of their youth? Since the age of youth is a little foolish and despised, is every advantage lost for that reason? Or is it because in their capriciousness they cannot keep friends or possessions? Yet all human endeavors, especially those pertaining to wealth, require time for their acquisition. Or is it because music is opposed to prudence, as wealth demands great prudence in its retention and especially in its disposition, or because those who had been poor from the beginning have worked hard to become accomplished, yet only improve their poverty with difficulty? Or does this happen in our territories because of the great number of musicians? For in various ways their practice and employment is hindered, so that they are frequently without work. A musician has so many obstacles, so much time is required for practice that produces weariness rather than pleasure. Something is always lacking, the perfection that is a necessary end, and consequently material gain. Or is it because those who take pleasure in the art are foolish adolescents who have little money and who are not equipped to go into other activities that are more physical in nature?[37]

Virtually all of Cardano's discussion of music seems to be related to art music. Perhaps his failure to give us more observations on entertainment music can be found in his admission,

> I was useless in conversation and entertainment and this was also one of the reasons why I avoided large banquets.[38]

But there is one reference to popular music which is rather interesting.

> This was the manner of singing songs in ancient times, also practiced now by strolling players in the market, when with lyre in hand they raise and lower its tones through only three or four intervals.[39]

---

[37] Ibid., 207.

[38] Quoted in Ore, *Cardano the Gambling Scholar*, 27.

[39] Miller, *Hieronymus Cardanus, Writings on Music*, 122.

Erasmus on Music

ON THE SUBJECT OF MUSIC, Erasmus is a considerable disappointment. Although he studied music with Obrecht[1] and apparently could play the viol,[2] his references to music, and there are many, tend to be passive and dispassionate. Most curious is that his identity with Humanism does not extend to include music.

His great mind is demonstrated in his wide knowledge of the literature on music, but it is not employed in original thinking on the nature of music. In this regard he will include important thoughts taken from the Greek philosophers, but offer the reader no explanation at all of their meaning. Some examples are:

> The composer who would set a serious subject to soft Lydian airs would be absurd.[3]
>
> ......
>
> There is more pleasure in hearing an old song than a new one, even if it is a better one.[4]
>
> ......
>
> A flute player produces sounds that are not his.[5]

He quotes the great testimonials of music found in ancient literature, but sometimes he seems to miss their true meaning and sometimes he distorts them. Take for example one of the most famous Greek myths, the story of Orpheus taming wild beasts, stones and trees with music. The purpose of the myth was to illustrate that music can affect and improve the nature of man. Erasmus, who surely knew better, offers two outrageously false explanations:

> Take those wild men sprung from hard rocks and oak trees—what power brought them together into a civilized society if not flattery? This is all that's meant by the lyre of Amphion and Orpheus.[6]
>
> ......
>
> The same poets record that Orpheus, poet and lute player, moved the hardest of stones with his singing. What did they mean? They meant to show that men as unfeeling as stone, who were living after the manner of wild beasts, were rescued from promiscuity by this wise and eloquent hero and initiated into the holy ways of marriage.[7]

---

1   *The Dodecachordon of Heinrich Glarean*, ed. Clement Miller (American Institute of Musicology, 1965), II, 252. Glarean says he heard this from Erasmus himself.
2   P.E. Hallett, *The Life and Illustrious Martyrdom of Sir Thomas More* (London, 1928), 15.
3   'Parallels,' [1514] quoted in *The Collected Works of Erasmus* (Toronto: University of Toronto Press, 1992), XXIII, 179.
4   Ibid., XXIII, 273.
5   Ibid., XXIII, 168. Early philosophers sometimes said the flute made the music, not the player.
6   'Praise of Folly,' [1503] in Ibid., XXVII, 101.
7   'On the Writing of Letters,' [1522] in Ibid., XXV, 135.

It is clear that to some degree Erasmus was still thinking of music in the old medieval definition as a branch of mathematics, as was still taught in the major universities. In a discussion of the Greek proverb, 'Double diapason,' Erasmus gets carried away, admitting 'I have rashly—and as it were forgetting myself—gone further into musical matters than the nature of the work undertaken required.' While he rarely writes of music in detail, these pages clearly reflect his knowledge of the old Scholastic mathematics based theories of music, as well as the principal earlier treatises such as Boethius. Erasmus defines the common usage of this proverb to mean any two things very far apart. In the course of his musical discussion he seeks to make the principal point that the range of two octaves is a kind of natural furthermost limit, with respect to the ear hearing the mathematical proportions in music. Clearly concerned that he was sticking his neck out, he tells us that as he was writing, a famous philosopher, Ambrogio Leone of Nola, just happened to walk in and thus he attributes to this man the remainder of the discussion. Leone finds two reasons for calling the double octave the natural limit. First, he has observed that the [male] voice cannot reach beyond the fifteenth without becoming forced and artificial. The second argument is because Reason and the senses must work together. While Reason can comprehend numbers of any size, for example the possibility of a distance of a thousand octaves, the senses do not distinguish relationships beyond two octaves.

> But the physical senses have had their own limits prescribed for them by nature, and if they transgress these, they gradually become misty and wandering, and can no longer judge with certainty as they used to do, but through a cloud, as they say, or in a dream. It was not fitting that principles of art should be drawn from an uncertainty of judgment. But since the ancients understood that beyond the fifteenth note of the scale the judgment of the ears began to fail, they decided to fix the bounds of harmony there, so that no one could have any reason to bring up that adage of yours, 'unheard music is useless.'[8]

We suspect that it was this association with mathematics which caused Erasmus to think of music as being somewhat exclusive. In a series of objections to a treatise by Latomus, Erasmus adds, for example, that 'mathematics, metaphysics and music' are not needed by everyone, as for instance the baker and the tailor.[9] And it may have been the association with mathematics, with its world of order and exactness, that caused Erasmus on two occasions to connect music with the divine. In one case Erasmus writes that he found in the works of Augustine a reference (which cannot be identified today) which mentions the Greek philosopher, Zeno, saying that the soul itself is a 'self-moving harmony, and for this reason can be caught up and carried away by harmonious things.' Erasmus adds a comment which seems to suggest a divinely implanted understanding of music.

---

[8] 'Adages,' in Ibid., XXXI, 202ff. Erasmus discusses the last phrase in a discussion of the proverb, 'Hidden music has no listeners [and is thus worthless].' [Ibid., XXXII, 117ff.]

[9] 'Apology Refuting Rumors and Suspicions ... by Latomus,' in Ibid., LXXI, 47.

[This is its nature] just as children too are affected by the modes of music through some natural affinity, even when they have no idea what music is.[10]

The other instance is a rather special case, for it is really one of the only documents which suggests that Erasmus was capable of being profoundly moved by music and the only place in all of his writings where he mentions any contemporary musician by name. This is a poem written in honor of Ockeghem a little more than a year after his death. Here Erasmus declares, 'Music is something divine.'

> Has it fallen silent then, that voice once so renowned, the golden voice of Ockeghem? Is the glory of music thus snuffed out? Sing, Apollo, come sing a sad dirge to your lyre. You also, Calliope, clad in mourning together with your sisters, pour forth loving tears. Mourn, all who are enraptured by the sweet pursuit of music, and extol this man with your praises. That sacred Phoenix of Apollo's art is dead.
>
> What are you doing, O envious Death? The golden voice has been silenced, the golden voice of Ockeghem, the voice that could move even stones, the voice that so often resounded in the vaulted nave with fluid and subtly modulated melodies, soothing the ears of the saints in heaven and likewise piercing the hearts of earthborn men.
>
> What are you doing, O envious Death? You are unjust precisely because you deal justly with everyone. It would be enough for you to take away indiscriminately the things that belong to mankind. Music is something divine. Why do you violate the divine?[11]

We suspect that for Erasmus the primary purpose of music was that of simple pleasure and leisure, something which he mentions many times. In a letter of 1519 for example, he seems to suggest by inference that music and reading are to be thought of as leisure, apart from the important things such as business.

> For it would be unwise in a man born for public affairs to gather dust by constant meditation in the company of what they call dumb teachers; on the contrary, just as Plato molds the spirit of his citizens by a judicious mixture of music and gymnastics, so the lives of great men should be kept in balance by interchanging leisure for study and the business of public affairs.[12]

---

[10] 'Adages,' in Ibid., XXXI, 167.
[11] 'An Epitaph for the Superlative Musician Jan Ockeghem,' in Ibid., LXXXV, 77.
[12] Letter to Guillaume de Croy [1519], in Ibid., VI, 339ff.

In another letter of the same year, when he is discussing the attitude of the Catholic conservatives turning against the humanities, he again seems to join music with simple and temporary pleasures.

> I have never seen anything more determined than this conspiracy against humane studies. Food and drink, sleep, music and dancing—of all such pleasures one can have enough, as Homer says; but the love of mischief-making in these men is never satisfied.[13]

A Greek proverb which Erasmus discusses is 'Singers tell many lies.' Of this, he says,

> It comes from the fact that singers, whose only object is to delight and give pleasure, produce for the most part what redounds to the credit of the audience [even though it is not true]; for nothing is more solemn than the truth, or more agreeable than flattery.[14]

His most interesting comment of this sort is regarding the Greek proverb, 'A wooer's life.' Erasmus says this represents a life of fastidious luxury, or 'A life of pure music.'[15]

The principal purpose of music found in most medieval literature is to soothe the listener. Erasmus first mentions this in an early poem of 1489.

> O brainless blockhead,
> you have need of the very Muse you reject.
> See how she confronts madness, soothes
> cruel-hearted savagery, subdues the demon.
> Since all these apply to you, hold poetry dear;
> take up once more the soothing lyre.[16]

Erasmus refers to this purpose twice in his book called 'Parallels,' and they are both quite interesting.

> They say that the tigress, if she hears the roll of drums all round her, is driven mad, and ends by tearing herself in pieces; even so, some people cannot stand what raises the spirits of others, as music, eloquence, and so forth.[17]
>
> ......
>
> As some magnets attract iron, but the themedes, which is found in Ethiopia, rejects and repels it, so there is one kind of music that calms the passions and another that rouses them.[18]

---

[13] Letter to Richard Pace [1519], in Ibid., VI, 354. The editors suggest that the Homer reference is to the *Illiad*, xiii, 636.

[14] 'Adages,' in Ibid., XXXIII, 128. In another place [Ibid., XXXIII, 281] he writes of the proverb, 'The aulos player of Tenedos,' who lied in a law suit.

[15] 'Adages,' in Ibid., XXXIV, 116.

[16] 'A Defense ... against Barbarous Persons ...,' in Ibid., LXXXV, 185. In this poem he also speaks of the Greek myths of music, as well as the tributes by early Latin poets.

[17] 'Parallels,' [1514] in Ibid., XXIII, 175.

[18] Ibid., XXIII, 225.

The purpose of music most emphasized by the ancient Greek philosophers was its capacity to affect the character of the listener. Erasmus discusses this idea, together with music therapy, in a lengthy letter to Pope Adrian VI in 1522. The subject of the letter was a new publication on the Psalms by the celebrated teacher of rhetoric, Arnobius. Erasmus begins with a lengthy metaphor in which he characterizes Arnobius as the harp of David. Of note here is a phrase which suggests, however indirectly, that Erasmus recognized that good music was not only sweet, but had emotions [fire].

> This instrument produces not merely animating notes that are sweet in the ears of pious folk; it has its fire as well.[19]

Erasmus then proceeds to his major discussion, which includes the extraordinary metaphor of Jesus on the cross representing a harp.

> To expel this vast contagion of moral corruption we need powerful spells, and some sort of enchanter, a master of his art, who can charm wisely. For this purpose I have provided almost a new weapon, not that the Psalms of David did not exist, but for most people they lay silent. It is a property, they say, of man-made music that it can either rouse the emotions or control them if a skilled performer makes an appropriate use of specific harmonies. It is said that Timotheus could kindle the heart of Alexander of Macedon with warlike fire by playing in certain particular modes. Pythagoras, by playing spondees in the Phrygian mode, transformed a young man mad with love and restored his sanity. A similar story is told of Empedocles, who is said by the use of some particular musical modes to have recalled to his proper wits a young man already beside himself with rage and hell-bent on murder. The tales told in antiquity of Mercury and Orpheus playing on the lyre look like fables; and yet these fictions were inspired by the wonders music can perform. Certainly Terpander and Arion in Lesbos and in Ionia are said by the historians to have cured many serious diseases as a regular thing by the use of musical harmonies. Ismenias of Thebes in Boeotia is recorded as relieving the torments of many sufferers from gout in the hip with appropriate melodies. When Virgil says that 'the clammy snake in the meadows is burst by the singing of spells,' this might be ignored as merely the utterance of a poet, had not our own Scriptures mentioned the charmer who charms so wisely and the adder that will not listen. David used his harp to come to the aid of Saul, whenever he was vexed by an evil spirit from the Lord.
>
> If then man-made music has such power to change the affections of both body and soul, how much more effective we must suppose this heavenly and divine music to be in purging our hearts of spiritual diseases and the evil spirits of this present world! Ambition is an overmastering disease, ill will and jealousy are a most evil spirit; and the majority of Christians are victims of this kind of plague, even those being often not exempt whose duty it was to cure their fellow men. The pagans of old possessed 'both words and spells,' with which they could 'of their distemper lose the greater part, and soothe the gnawing canker of the heart.' And surely Christ's music has words and spells with which we can charm out of our hearts the love of things transient and charm into its place the love of heavenly things. Pythagoras commanded musical modes whereby he could recall to sanity a young man beside himself with infatuation; and does not the Christian psalmist command modes whereby he can recall to the love of peace the princes who are endlessly at loggerheads in these most crazy wars? But we must first use this music to cure ourselves before we attempt to cure other men's diseases. There is no part of the Holy Scripture that does not have these powerful modes at its com-

---

19 Letter to Adrian VI [1522], in Ibid., IX, 145ff.

mand, provided that we do not stop up our ears like deaf adders for fear that the strong magic of the divine enchanter may penetrate into our hearts. But in my view no modes are more powerful than the music of the Psalms; for in this book it was the will of that divine spirit to lay up a store for us of his most secret and delightful mysteries; and in it he enshrined certain musical modes of greatest power, by which we might be changed into a frame of mind worthy of Christ, provided only that there is someone at hand who can wake the strings of this psaltery with proper skill.

This is the special duty of bishops and priests; and yet every individual might learn to play for himself. The spirit will help him as he plucks the strings and will breathe secret power into his inmost parts, if only he provides a pure and fervent heart—the ears, that is, with which a mind that has been purified can listen. Oh that your Holiness might be our new David—that consummate master of this kind of music!—who not only played himself but taught many other singers to do the same. And David was a prototype of Jesus Christ, our psalmist, who, when his body was strung like a harp upon the cross, played nothing common, nothing earthly, but such a melodious music as the Father loves, the moving force of which we feel. What harmony of the divine love sounded in that chord: 'Father, forgive them, for they know not what they do!'

The world too has its instruments, but their infernal notes return an unlovely sound. How speak the strings of anger? 'Revenge and rapine, Cast them out, Cut them down!' What tune does ambition play? 'On, on! extend your realm, think not of oaths nor of religion, when dominion is the prize.' What twangling notes we hear from avarice! 'You see no man is happy save him who has great possessions; by fair means or by foul get, get and pile and keep!' How sound the chords of luxury and lust? 'Live now to please yourself, for you know not what your portion will be after this life.' No less discordant are the chords played by jealousy and spite. This is of course the music of the world, which by such dreadful strains calls up pestilential appetites within us, and like the Sirens lures us to destruction with notes as sweet as they are fatal. This is the music that intoxicates and maddens us, and so we fight wars, we raise rebellion, we are ambitious, greedy, wrathful, and vindictive; we bite each other and are bitten in turn.

The only other lengthy discussion by Erasmus on the subject of the effect of music on a person's character is found in a treatise on Christian marriage. Here, curiously, he seems to focus only on the negative implications of this characteristic.

> It is customary now among some nations to compose every year new songs which young girls study assiduously. The subject matter of the songs is usually the following: a husband deceived by his wife, or a daughter guarded in vain by her parents, or a clandestine affair of lovers. These things are presented as if they were wholesome deeds, and a successful act of profligacy is applauded. Added to pernicious subject matter are such obscene innuendoes, expressed in metaphors and allegories, that no manner of depravity could be depicted more vilely.
>
> Many earn a livelihood in this occupation, especially among the Flemish. If laws were enforced, composers of such common ditties would be flogged for singing these doleful songs to the licentious. Men who publicly corrupt youth are making a living from crime, yet parents are found who think it a mark of good breeding if their daughters know such songs.
>
> Antiquity considered music to belong to the liberal disciplines. Since musical sounds have great power to affect the soul of man ... the ancients carefully distinguished musical modes, preferring the Dorian to others. They believed this matter to be so important that laws were enacted so that music would not be permitted in the state if it corrupted the minds of citizens.

> But in our music, apart from obscenity in texts and subjects, how much is frivolity, how much is folly? There existed in former times a kind of performance in which, without words and only by pantomime, anything that was desired could be represented. In the same way in modern songs, even if the text is not sung, the foulness of the subject can be understood from the nature of the music. Then add to this the sound of frenetic pipes and noisy drums combining with a frenzy of movements. To such music young girls dance, to this they are accustomed, and yet we think there is no danger to their morals.[20]

While Erasmus rarely goes into detail regarding performance practice he might have observed, his brief comments often suggest a broad understanding. In one place, for example, he calls practice, 'the best teacher of any subject.' He follows this with the specific example, that one learns music by playing.[21] He seems inclined toward sensitivity when he observes, 'The melodiousness of harmony depends on the *quality* of the lute'[22] and 'musicians win our hearts with a light touch on the strings, not heavy pounding.'[23]

One value which he appears to suggest was considered important in the sixteenth century was accuracy. He refers to this in a discussion of the proverb, 'To strike the same wrong note.'

> Adopted from musicians, for whom it is a terrible thing to play a wrong note more than once on the same string. It can well be said of those who frequently go wrong in the same matter, or commit the same fault over and over again. The first lapse may be ascribed to chance or rashness, but to do it again argues stupidity or inexperience.[24]

Another place where Erasmus seems to argue for expertise in music is in his explanation of the Greek proverb, 'When you're offered turtle-meat, either eat or do not eat,' which means do not do anything half-way. He then adds the thought,

> Remember how many activities there are which are admirable if you throw yourself into them, and do harm if you are lukewarm; or which do not admit of mediocrity, like music and poetry.[25]

A few comments suggest Erasmus had a particular sensitivity to inaccuracy in singers.

> Singers often take little trouble when singing in chorus in the theater, but put them into competition with one another and every note is studied.[26]

......

---

[20] Erasmus, *Opera omnia*, ed. J. Clericus (Leiden, 1703–1706), V, 717F, quoted in Clement A. Miller, 'Erasmus on Music,' *The Musical Quarterly* 52, no. 3 (July, 1966): 347ff, http://www.jstor.org/stable/3085961

[21] 'Adages,' in *The Collected Works of Erasmus*, XXXII, 25.

[22] 'Puerpera' [1526], in *The Colloquies of Erasmus*, trans. Craig Thompson (Chicago: University of Chicago Press, 1965), 280.

[23] 'Parallels,' [1514] in *The Collected Works of Erasmus*, XXIII, 136.

[24] 'Adages,' in Ibid., XXXI, 393.

[25] Ibid., XXXII, 260.

[26] 'Parallels,' [1514] in Ibid., XXIII, 189ff.

> When a singer has a flute accompaniment, he can make many mistakes which his audience does not detect.[27]

Erasmus seems to have held instrumentalists in some awe, if not resentment, for the amount of money they were paid. In a discussion of the hiring of teachers for children, Erasmus says in passing,

> Flute players and trumpeters by the dozen are maintained with huge salaries, yet no one more rightly deserves a large and attractive salary than a learned schoolmaster.[28]

In several places Erasmus, like nearly all humanists, is critical of polyphonic music. His strongest statement in this regard is found in his treatise, 'The Tongue.'

> The other liberal arts have also degenerated from their original simplicity, just like the morals of society. They have grown more fluent and less authentic; the loquacity of the declamatory schools has ruined eloquence. Again, what is more elaborate than present-day music, mimicking the chatter of many birds with such a large number of vocal parts. What would the Spartan ephor Emerepes say now? He was the man who cut away two of the nine strings from the lyre of Phrynis the musician with his axe, telling him not to ruin the art of music. Supposing he heard one and the same instrument imitating trumpets, horns, bugles, recorders descant, tenor, and alto, thunder, and the voices of men and birds in our houses of God? The standard of our music reflects that of our fashion in clothing and furnishings and architecture. The original simplicity has vanished, and elaborate caprices grow daily more common.[29]

But, on the other hand, in one place he seems to indicate a preference for multi-part music.

> Part-singing is more melodious than if everyone sang exactly the same note.[30]

In the general context of performance practice among singers, Erasmus makes some important associations between speech and music. His 'The Right Way of Speaking Latin and Greek' is interesting particularly in view of the belief of some modern philologists that speech developed from music. We also find fascinating the natural examples he supplies for a phenomenon by which the brain alters our perception of sounds, resulting, in the case of music, for the aesthetic necessity of making lower tones more pronounced.

> BEAR. Some people are so insensitive that they cannot distinguish accent from quantity, even though they are altogether different things. Striking a high note is not the same as holding a note, nor is stressing a sound the same as prolonging it ...

---

[27] 'Parallels,' [1514] in Ibid., XXIII, 177.

[28] 'On the Writing of Letters,' [1522] in Ibid., XXV, 23. He argues against any form of tenure for teachers, as well as against paying them too much.

> Otherwise there is danger that the same abuses will ensue that we observe in high priestly offices, where the more lucrative the position, the more unworthy the one who occupies it.

[29] 'The Tongue,' [1525] in Ibid., XXIX, 286ff.

[30] 'Parallels,' [1514] in Ibid., XXIII, 273.

> Yet anyone with a smattering of music can distinguish without any trouble the difference between long and short on the one hand and high and low on the other. And after all speaking is just an articulated sequence of voiced sound. Metrical principles exist in prose as well as in verse, even though the rules are less restrictive and definite. But if they are disregarded speech will no more be speech than singing would be singing if high and low, long and short, were indiscriminately muddled up. The accent can justifiably be called, as it was by some ancient grammarians, the soul of the word ... I think you play the guitar?
>
> LION. After a fashion.
>
> BEAR. Do you not often find yourself making a low note long or a high note short as well as the other way round?
>
> LION. Yes. Though the contrast is still more marked with wind instruments.
>
> BEAR. So why should we be so crude and unmusical when we talk, making every syllable that is accented high long and all the others short? Even donkeys could have taught us better. When they bray they take longer over the low note than over the high one.
>
> LION. The cuckoo does much the same.[31]

Erasmus continues this comparison of speech to music by mentioning that a speaker often begins slowly and then accelerates, as happens in music. When the question is raised regarding the relationship of short to long in syllables, the answer is given as one to two, although 'in ordinary speech there is no need to keep the ratio so exactly as there would be in choral singing or in dancing to a guitar.'[32]

In another treatise, Erasmus again compares speech and music and in one passage criticizes contemporary singers.

> For well-timed silence is a product of the same art as well-timed speech ... Singers who blunder during the rests that separate the vocal parts display their ignorance of music and suggest that they are not even singing their parts with artistic understanding.[33]

From his extensive reading of ancient literature, Erasmus mentions a number of aspects of performance in early literature which we have not found elsewhere. First, he describes some of the performance practices of the ancient lyre players, information to which he credits a first-century writer named Asconius Pedianus, although no such writing by Asconius is extant today.

> Ordinary lyre-players while playing make use of both hands, holding the plectrum in the left hand, which they call 'outside playing,' and plucking the strings with the fingers of the left hand, which they call 'inside.' It was thought difficult to do as the player, Aspendus, did, who never used both hands, but played everything—the music in its entirety—'inside,' and encompassed it all with the left hand only. In this way the piece was entirely performed by the left hand, which touched the strings

---

31 'The Right Way of Speaking Latin and Greek,' [1528] in Ibid., XXVI, 422ff.

32 Ibid., XXVI, 424. Later [Ibid., 428], Erasmus suggests that in speaking a distinction be made between high, accented syllables, and lower sounds which might be as much as a fourth, fifth or even an octave—although he admits this might be 'ungraceful.'

33 'The Tongue,' [1525] in Ibid., XXIX, 288.

silently and with a light action, so that the sound was audible only to the player or to a person very close to him. Hence came the proverb: thieving fellows were often called in Greek 'Aspendus lyre-players,' because they kept their thefts to themselves, as the players did their music.[34]

In a brief discussion of a proverb, 'What need was there to play on the long pipes,' Erasmus refers to Plutarch saying that in Egyptian tomb paintings the long flutes were primarily associated with religious rites.[35] We believe, however, that the tomb paintings picture the long flute used in broader circumstances. In his discussion of the proverb, 'Carian music,' Erasmus gives a detailed history of another instrument he associates with dirges, the 'Carian flute.'[36]

In discussing a proverb, 'From Dorian to Phrygian,' which meant any extreme change of manner, Erasmus mentions that he has found a unique reference in Apuleius who calls Dorian 'warlike.' Since he believed that Dorian was usually considered more delicate, he wonders if this reference meant the use of this mode to calm soldiers when on the way to battle. Then, regarding the general discussion of modes by the ancients, he adds,

> I myself suppose that the Ancients have given us different accounts of the systems of harmony, because the system itself changed with changes in the behavior of society. In the early days the people of Asia were reputed for their discipline, before they were softened by luxury. The same happened to the Spartans, among whom were Dorians. Hence those names for mixtures of mode, hypodorian, mixolydian and hypermixolydian.[37]

In discussing the proverb, 'Babys plays the [aulos] even worse,' Erasmus mentions a Greek myth we have not read.

> Babys, they say, was a brother of Marsyas, the man who was not afraid to challenge Apollo himself to a musical contest. When he was defeated, he was suspended by Apollo from a pine-tree upside down, and flayed. Then, when Apollo was preparing to destroy Babys too, Pallas interceded for him, saying that his aulos playing was so unsuccessful and unskillful that clearly he was quite negligible; 'Babys' she said 'plays even worse.' Apollo was impressed by her words, and treated Babys with such disdain that he did not even think him worthy of punishment, but judged it better to abandon him to his incompetence.[38]

Regarding the proverb, 'Hipparchion loses his voice,' Erasmus observes,

> They say that in Greece in the old days there were two leading lyre players, Hipparchion and Rufinus. At the regular games celebrated every nine years at Juliopolis these two were to engage in a contest; and it so happened that Hipparchion was unnerved by the uproar in the theater and lost his voice; hence this became a popular joke.[39]

---

34 'Adages,' in Ibid., XXXIII, 34.
35 Ibid., XXXI, 467.
36 Ibid., XXXII, 167.
37 'Adages,' in Ibid., XXXIII, 283ff.
38 Ibid., XXXIV, 18.
39 Ibid., XXXIV, 43.

Of the proverb, 'Moschus singing a Boeotian strain,' Erasmus, without giving a source, says Moschus was 'an unskillful lyre player [and singer], who used to stretch out a note to great lengths without drawing breath.' 'Boeotian,' he says was a mode like Dorian or Phrygian.[40]

Finally, he mentions an ancient gladiator's song, 'Not you I seek, 'tis fish I seek,' which he says he found in Sextus Festus.[41]

Erasmus rarely describes the actual performances of music which he heard, yet we know that during his travels he was serenaded by church choirs and civic wind bands.[42] He does, however, mention the importance of the listener, one of the chief hallmarks of art music. In a discussion of a proverb, 'A jackdaw has no business with a lute,' Erasmus characterizes this bird as very noisy and then adds, 'But the lute requires silence and attentive ears.'[43] He cites another proverb, 'The pig heard the trumpet,' which he associates with people 'who are neither pleased nor moved by what they hear.'[44]

He touches on the listener in another Greek proverb, 'You sing in vain,' which he says had its origin in singers who were unpleasing to their audience and therefore no one listened. Implied here is the idea that to give delight is the primary purpose. He also notes that this proverb can apply to lute players and here he is thinking of *sung* poetry, for he says this refers to lute-players, 'who sing without being paid anything.'[45]

In one place, however, Erasmus observes that such is the nature of music that the performer receives some pleasure even if there is no contemplative listener.

> Singing has its own delight, even when the person to whom the song is sung with the tender tones of love does not move a limb in response.[46]

In one interesting passage in his 'The Education of a Christian Prince,' Erasmus uses the analogy of music to demonstrate the importance of learning in early childhood. The additional point here is that *quality* music should be used with children.

> Pains will therefore have to be taken to accustom them from the outset to what is best, for any music sounds sweet to those who have become used to it. And nothing is harder than to withdraw someone from behavior which has already taken root in his character from habitual usage.[47]

---

[40] Ibid., XXXIV, 307.

[41] Quoted in a letter to Francois I [1523] in Ibid., X, 118.

[42] P. S. Allen, *Erasmus* (Oxford, 1934), 15.

[43] 'Adages,' in *The Collected Works of Erasmus*, XXXI, 346.

[44] Ibid.

[45] 'Adages,' in Ibid., XXXI, 377.

[46] Ibid., XXXI, 424. Earlier [Ibid., 84], Erasmus recalls a story by Aristotle of a flutist who was promised he would be paid more, the better he played. When he asked for his pay, he was told he had already been paid, as he had been repaid by his fine playing.

[47] 'The Education of a Christian Prince,' [1516] in Ibid., XXVII, 259.

Because of Erasmus' background in the church, we are not surprised to find that it is here that he writes with the most passion about music. His greatest joy in music seems to have been in hearing the Psalms.

> But it was heavenly music that inspired the man who wrote, 'How amiable are thy tabernacles, O Lord of hosts! My soul longeth, yea even fainteth for the courts of the Lord.' And again, 'My heart is like wax; it is melted in the midst of my bowels.' Such were the harmonies whose power had breathed upon the apostles when they said, 'Lord, whither shall we go? Thou hast the words of life.' Sweet and tuneful indeed is the concerted sound when love, chastity, sobriety, modesty, and the other virtues sing together in harmonious variety. And this music has different styles to suit different themes. In some which, mournful though they are, are pleasing in the ear of God, we lament our sins. Some give us strength and courage boldly to resist the devil. Some are cheerful and full of joy, to use when we give thanks to God for his goodness to us. Some are used to console and comfort the afflicted. In a word, this life offers no kind of trouble that we cannot easily endure, if, as St. Paul puts it in his letter to the Colossians, we instruct and admonish each other, with psalms and hymns of praise and spiritual songs singing gratefully in our hearts to the Lord, and if, whatever we do in word or deed, we do all in the name of the Lord Jesus, giving thanks to God and the Father through the Son. And this music will be the more pleasing to God if performed by a numerous choir in harmony of hearts and voices.
>
> But to return to the Psalms of David, no man can appreciate how sweet this music making is unless he has perceived its mystic meaning. What is the reason, otherwise, why so many monks and priests find it so tedious to intone these famous psalms? Surely because they sing them with their mouths, not with their minds. And if any of them have no time to turn the pages of long commentaries by other authors, such men, though hard to please, will find Arnobius a help, for his note is often shorter than the psalm itself, and if they read his brief disquisition they will have sung the psalm and learned its meaning at one stroke. All priests should therefore take special care to master once and for all what they sing every day. As a result they will find more comfort in one psalm which they have learned to understand and have sung with the mind, than in forty sung merely with the mouth. Of one thing above all others our would-be psalm singer must be perfectly convinced, that it was the purpose of the Holy Spirit, and a very wise purpose to, to wrap up the mysteries of heavenly wisdom under these layers of metaphor.[48]

Music history texts have failed to relate the full extent to which instruments were accompanying singers in the sixteenth-century churches. Erasmus mentions the use of instruments in the church frequently, although he evidently found little appreciation for this new style, preferring the old unaccompanied chant. He not only tells us that one customarily heard instruments accompany voices in village churches, but condemns this as a distraction to the Christian.

> From every quarter of the world music of every style rises from every kind of instrument to assault the ears of the Blessed Virgin, who hears every day the song of the angelic choirs—unless I am mistaken, a far sweeter song than ours. It is only because men listen often to the din of voices and the noise of instruments and never or rarely to the message of the gospel that in our villages and even in some of our towns there is such naivete and such ignorance of the Christian faith.[49]

---

[48] Letter to Adrian VI [1522], Ibid., IX, 145ff.

[49] Letter to Thiebaut Bietry [1525], in Ibid., XI, 106.

Erasmus mentions the use of instruments again, among other objections, in the course of a discussion of I Corinthians 14.

> In some countries the whole day is now spent in endless singing, yet one worthwhile sermon exciting true piety is hardly heard in six months ... not to mention the kind of music that has been brought into divine worship, in which not a single word can be clearly understood. Nor is there a free moment for singers to contemplate what they are singing.
>
> What else is heard in monasteries, colleges, and almost all churches, besides the clamor of voices? Yet in St. Paul's time there was no song, only speech. Later song was accepted by posterity, but it was nothing else than a distinct and modulated speech (such as we presently use in the Lord's Prayer), which the congregation understood and to which it responded. But what more does it hear now than meaningless sounds?
>
> At present there is no end of psalms, songs, festal music, and dirges, from which we imagine we gain spiritual merit. And what is more serious, in the maintenance of these services, priests are bound by almost tighter chains than they are to Christ's teachings. The people are compelled to attend and thus are taken away from their labors. How are they to support their families, and what activity could be more meritorious? ...
>
> We have brought into sacred edifices a certain elaborate and theatrical music, a confused interplay of diverse sounds, such as I do not believe was ever heard in Greek or Roman theaters. Straight trumpets, curved trumpets, pipes and sambucas resound everywhere, and vie with human voices. Amorous and shameful songs are heard, the kind to which harlots and mimes dance. People flock to church as to a theater for aural delight.
>
> To this end organists are maintained at large salaries, and crowds of children spend every summer in practicing such warblings, meanwhile studying nothing of value. The dregs of humanity, the vile and the unreliable (as a great many are drunken revelers), are kept on salary, and because of this pernicious custom the church is burdened with heavy expenses. I ask you to consider, how many paupers, dying in want, could be supported on the salaries of singers?
>
> These activities are so pleasing to monks, especially the English, that they perform nothing else. Their song should be mourned; they think God is pleased with ornamental neighings and agile throats. In this custom also in the Benedictine Colleges in Britain where young boys, adolescents, and professional singers are supported, who sing the morning service to the Virgin mother with a very melodious interweaving of voices and organs ...
>
> Those who are more doltish than really learned in music are not content on feast days unless they use a certain distorted kind of music called *Fauburdum*. This neither gives forth the preexisting melody nor observes the harmonies of the art. In addition, when temperate music is used in church in this way, so that the meaning of the words may more easily come to the listener, it also seems a fine thing to some if one or other part, intermingled with the rest, produces a tremendous tonal clamor, so that not a single word is understood. Thus the whims of the foolish are indulged and their baser appetites are satisfied.[50]

A similar attack on Church music of his time includes a qualified endorsement of polyphonic music.

> I was not speaking as much about any kind of ecclesiastical song as about unseemly music and alluring songs which the whims of naive women or simple men have added to religious services.

---

[50] Erasmus, *Opera omnia*, ed. J. Clericus (Leiden, 1703–1706), VI, 731C-732C, quoted in Clement A. Miller, 'Erasmus on Music,' *The Musical Quarterly* 52, no. 3 (July, 1966): 338ff, http://www.jstor.org/stable/3085961

> Clamorers are so named because presently in many churches and monasteries, by thundering forth in a raucous bellowing, they so fill up the church that all sounds are obscured and nothing can be understood …
>
> I call booming the nearly warlike sound of organs, straight trumpets, curved trumpets, horns, and also bombards, since these too are accepted in religious services …
>
> But my judgment differs very much from those who condemn proper church song. I do not dispute about current polyphonic music if it is used with moderation and discretion.[51]

Finally, he complains of the use of instruments even during Vespers,

> which are done with the most ornate harmonies of singers and organs, and also trumpets, since they too are often heard in church in songs and prayers of psalmody.[52]

In spite of these attacks on the use of instruments in the Church, in three places Erasmus takes the opposite view in recommending these instruments in praise of the Lord. The first is an early (1499) poem written to celebrate Easter.

> Let that choir sing a heavenly melody;
> we on earth will applaud and mingle our
> earthly instruments with our weak voices. Let
> one strike his harp; let another pluck the
> resounding strings. Let one sing to the lyre; let
> another shake the jiggling tambourine. From
> one side let the blown horn sound; from
> another let the sweet flute blend its smooth
> notes, making music for the triumphant
> procession of the Lord.[53]

The second of these is found in a letter to William Roper, for whom Erasmus expresses the wish that he will have children. Erasmus recommends he sing of Jesus to the baby,

> to your lyre instead of nursery rhymes to please your little ones. For [Jesus] alone is worthy to be praised continually on the strings and pipe, with songs and every sort of music-making.[54]

We have quoted some of Erasmus' views on the correspondence of speech and music. He returns to this subject in the context of contemporary Church choral singing.

> You know how they vary the pace of their singing, sometimes to double time, sometimes to triple, according to certain proportions or measures as they are now called. But there is no need in our case for this degree of discrimination. The point will be clear if you just conform with musical terminology to the extent of dividing breves into semi-breves …

---

[51] Ibid., 340.

[52] Ibid., 341. In another place [*Opera omnia*, V, 718C], Erasmus complains that the instrumentalists sometimes 'converse together in the impudent manner of singers' during the service.

[53] 'A Heroic Poem on the Feast of Easter,' in *The Collected Works of Erasmus*, LXXXV, 309.

[54] 'Commentary on Prudentius' Hymn,' [1524] in Ibid., XXIX, Dedicatory Letter, 173.

> In my view though, the real difficulty in observing them is where one has many voices, particularly untrained voices, in unisons, and I imagine this must be why church choirs do not differentiate even between long and short when singing psalms and canticles, and indeed pay scant attention to differences of accent, but speak together in equal time units so that there is no getting out of step with each other or unseemly confusion introduced by varying vowel lengths. Even in hymns, where different lengths are put on different vowels, this is not done according to the natural lengths of the syllables, but by arbitrary arrangement. The stricter orders, though, do not admit this form of singing, and all their utterance is in spondees. But in my view Ambrose must have ordered his hymns to be sung with full regard for the differences between syllables, and I do not doubt that this was in fact how they were sung until the spread of illiteracy.[55]

Erasmus appears to have been opposed to congregational singing, especially after the model of the enthusiastic congregational singing of the early Christians. Better to leave the singing to the Church professionals.

> In early times the entire congregation sang and responded Amen to the priest. The consequent thunderous noise and ridiculous confusion of voices produced a spectacle unworthy of divine worship. In our day those who are appointed sing fittingly and the rest sing to the Lord [only] in their hearts.[56]

He was also opposed to the growing length and importance of Church music.

> The Creed is shortened, the Lord's Prayer is not heard, and the singing of the prosa detains the congregation a full half hour. Added to this song are melismas [*caudae vocum*] which are just as long or even longer.[57]

And to any singing which is not strictly liturgical.

> Likewise ... the song now used in some churches for peace or against pestilence, or for a successful harvest, can be omitted without detriment to religious devotion.[58]

Erasmus was obviously bothered by the fact that many Church leaders were no longer simple, pious men, but lived in extravagance like secular princes. He satirizes this at some length in a witty little tract called 'Julius Excluded from Heaven.' Here we find the deceased pope, Julius II, finding the gates of heaven locked and being interrogated by the first pope, St. Peter. At one point Julius is telling Peter how much better the life of a pontiff is these days, and by way of example describes his own triumphal entry into Bologna.

> If you'd seen the ponies, the horses, the columns of armed soldiers, the panoply of the generals, the displays of hand-picked boys, the torches gleaming on all sides, the sumptuous litters, the procession of bishops, the stately cardinals, the trophies, the spoils; if you'd heard the cheers of people and

---

[55] 'The Right Way of Speaking Latin and Greek,' [1528] in Ibid., XXVI, 427.

[56] Erasmus, *Opera omnia*, ed. J. Clericus (Leiden, 1703–1706), V, 959E, quoted in Clement A. Miller, 'Erasmus on Music,' *The Musical Quarterly* 52, no. 3 (July, 1966): 334, http://www.jstor.org/stable/3085961

[57] Ibid., 336.

[58] Ibid., 336.

soldiers resounding to the sky, the sound of applause echoing all round, the music of trumpets, the thunder of cornets ... and myself, the leader and prime mover of the whole pageant, carried on high like some god.[59]

He is critical of high Church leaders in another place where he complains that the Church princes will only offer their services for a fee, observing, 'without pay they sing no psalms.'[60]

Many early writers remark on the fear caused by the sound of the trumpet, for it was so identified with battle. According to Erasmus there was a Latin proverb, 'Ante tubam trepidas,' referring to those who were frightened even before they heard the trumpet play.[61]

Erasmus describes a police action against a criminal mob, known as the Black Band, in Germany when a trumpet signal was mistakenly sounded prematurely, resulting in confusion during which more than a thousand person were 'cut to pieces.'[62] In one of the poems of his 'Epigrammata,' Erasmus mentions the watchman's trumpet. In a kind of reverse reference to the 'Music of the Spheres,' he says the watchman 'sends his shrill trumpet notes up to the stars.'[63]

In one of many passages which reflect both the hostility Erasmus felt for the Jews and the dislike he had for the military trumpet, he makes the point that the birth of Jesus was announced not by trumpets, but by singing.

> When Christ was born, did the angels sound trumpets of war? The Jews heard the noise of the trumpet, for they were permitted to wage war, and this was the appropriate sign for men whose law told them to hate their enemies. But the angels of peace sing a very different song in the ears of a people seeking peace.[64]

It is difficult to imagine the somber Erasmus enjoying popular entertainment, something, indeed, which he rarely mentions. When he does mention it, it is usually a criticism of some sort and between the lines we always clearly see his own prejudices, as in this comment on hunting.

> In the same category belong those who care for nothing but hunting wild game, and declare they take unbelievable pleasure in the hideous blast of the hunting horn and baying of the hounds. Dogs' dung smells sweet as cinnamon to them, I suppose, and what delicious satisfaction when the beast is to be dismembered![65]

---

59 'Julius Excluded from Heaven,' in *The Collected Works of Erasmus*, XXVII, 192ff.
60 'Adages,' in Ibid., XXXII, 186.
61 Ibid., XXXIV, 77.
62 Details are found in letters to Thomas More and Cuthbert Tunstall [both of 1518], in Ibid.,V, 401, 409.
63 'The Castle Commonly called Hammes,' in Ibid., LXXXV, 51.
64 'A Complaint of Peace Spurned and Rejected by the Whole World,' [1516] in Ibid., XXVII, 300. Erasmus mentions the loud trumpets of war again in his colloquy, 'Militaria.' [1522]
65 'Praise of Folly,' [1503] in Ibid., XXVII, 112.

Erasmus' lack of respect for professional entertainers is quite clear in his discussion of the Latin proverb, 'Once a buffoon, never an honest family man.'

> The meaning is that a man who has once lost all sense of shame, and with complete disregard for his reputation has taken to playing the buffoon in public, will scarcely ever return to respectability ... Fortune often showers wealth on the unworthy, but good character and good sense is not hers to give.[66]

In his discussion of the proverb, 'From horses to asses,' which refers to one's moving to a lower profession, the examples which Erasmus provides usually includes an entertainer as the lowest class. For example, a philosopher becoming a 'ballad-singer' and a blacksmith turned strolling player.[67]

We find in Erasmus only an occasional reference to the entertainment music heard at banquets. In discussing a proverb, 'You deserve no praise, even at a feast,' Erasmus recalls that in ancient Greece lyre players often sang of gods and famous men at almost every feast. He suggests, however, that often these performances were primarily for the entertainment of the audience.[68] Another reference makes it clear that most music heard on these occasions was intended for entertainment.

> Where pleasure's the object, the worst speaker deserves praise no less than the best, because he's no less entertaining; just as the only singer who gives pleasure is one who sings exceptionally well or exceptionally badly.[69]

The type of entertainment music heard seems to have varied greatly. An early poem, composed in 1490, describes rather elegant music.

> They do not care what aromas rise from the
> fully laden banquet tables or what vintage
> wines foam in full cups or what an abundance
> of song is plucked from melodious strings or
> what endless airs float about from lovely flutes.[70]

But a character in one of Erasmus' colloquies speaks of a much different kind of music.

> I disagree emphatically with those who think a dinner party isn't fun unless it overflows with silly, bawdy stories and rings with dirty songs.[71]

---

[66] 'Adages,' in Ibid., XXXIII, 195.
[67] 'Adages,' in Ibid., XXXII, 83.
[68] Ibid., XXXIV, 8.
[69] 'Convivium fabulosum' [1524], in *The Colloquies of Erasmus*, 256.
[70] 'An Elegiac Poem on Patience,' in *The Collected Works of Erasmus*, LXXXV, 253.
[71] 'Convivium religiosum' [1522], in *The Colloquies of Erasmus*, 56.

Good music or bad, we can't imagine our somber Erasmus having much fun at any of these banquets.

> Ask a wise man to dinner and he'll upset everyone by his gloomy silence or tiresome questions ... Haul him off to a public entertainment and his face will be enough to spoil the people's enjoyment.[72]

---

[72] 'Praise of Folly,' [1503] in Ibid., XXVII, 101. This, perhaps Erasmus' most famous work, was an attempt to make serious points in a humorous context. However, his very strong and pointed comments about nearly every level of society, even the pope, caused the book to be repeatedly condemned and won numerous enemies.

The Academies

WHILE THIS BOOK consists of the views and comments on music by some of the most important individuals of the Renaissance, it is important to remember that the Renaissance itself had at its heart a return to the importance of the individual man, in contrast to the medieval position that it was the Church which mattered and who would speak for all men. With the new focus on man it followed that groups of men began to meet to discuss mutual topics of interest. Those gatherings which were composed mostly of men were known as Academies, the earliest of which known to us is the 387 BC one founded by Plato in Athens where he taught and lectured on philosophy and the sciences until his death. The school continued until the sixth century AD when it was closed by the emperor Justinian, who declared it a 'pagan' school.

The best-known resurrection of the name was an academy founded in Florence by Marsilio Ficino (1433–1499), a man who devoted himself to the translation of the works of Plato and in general developing himself as a 'Renaissance man.' Thus, apart from the academy he founded, he was known as a scholar, doctor, musician and priest. He was also active in several of the 'weird sciences,' including astrology. He was much in demand for creating horoscopes and it is said that one he did for a child, Giovanni, of the Medici predicted the child would one day become a pope. In fact he did become Leo X, who, by the way, was created a pope before he became a priest. His practice of medicine was based in large part on the 'Humors,' thus his biographer, Giovanni Corsi, writing just after the death of Ficino, combines these 'sciences' in the following:

> [Ficino's] health was not at all settled, for he suffered very much from a weakness of the stomach, and although he always appeared cheerful and festive in company, yet it was thought that he sat long in solitude and became as if numb with melancholy. This came about either from black bile produced by the excessive burning of bile through continual night study, or, as he himself said, from Saturn, which at his birth was in the ascendant in Aquarius and nearly square to Mars in Scorpio.[1]

Ficino was a tutor to the great Lorenzo de' Medici and his academy enjoyed the participation of not only Lorenzo, but also several great names of the Florentine Renaissance, including Alberti, Poliziano and Pico della Mirandola. The meetings of Ficino's academy were concerned with the discussion of philosophy and it was here that he contributed to Humanism. Following his interpretation of Plato, Ficino took the position of establishing the importance of the study of Man, himself. It is difficult to describe for readers today how significant a departure from the Church dogma this was. For more than one thousand years the Church

---

[1] Giovanni Corsi, *The Life of Marsilio Ficino* (Faculty, Language Department, School of Economic Science, London).

had basically taken the position that they would tell man how to think. Once you establish the unique importance of the individual man, you have greatly complicated the role of the Church.

But we do not mean to suggest that there was a hostile relationship between Ficino's academy and the Church, for Ficino, as a priest, imagined a close association. He viewed the poet as a kind of prophet, in so far as he was divinely inspired.

> All those who have invented anything great in any of the nobler arts did so especially when they took refuge in the citadel of the Soul.[2]

It was in this frame of understanding that Ficino also spoke of love, that love is more effective than the intellect in search of truth and that 'Love is the Teacher and Ruler of the Arts.'[3]

But, as we said, Ficino's academy played a role in the humanist movement and it was from this perspective that they played an influence on developments in the field of music. Ficino, himself was a performing musician, observed,

> Our century like a golden age restored to light the liberal arts that were nearly extinct: grammar, poetry, rhetoric, painting, sculpture, architecture, music and the ancient performance of songs with the Orphic lyre.[4]

Because both the Italian and French intellectuals had taken from the ancient Greek writers a concept of music being closely related to the unseen organization of the world, it is no surprise that for them music included poetry and vice versa. In the Catholic countries, however, many writers held to the Church position that the words are the important thing, not the music. Ficino subscribed to the ancient Greek belief that music was important for helping the soul to retune itself to the cosmic, or divine, harmony. No doubt it was believed that this could be observed regularly in performance. A later French philosopher, Pontus de Tyard, who was much influenced by Ficino, used to tell of a banquet in Milan when,

> a lute player ravished the guests utterly out of themselves by his divinely languorous playing; and then, by a more vigorous tune, restored to them the souls which he had before stolen.[5]

However, for Ficino himself it was clear that the greater affect on man came from the poetry.

> But poetry is superior to music, since through the words it speaks not only to the ear but also directly to the mind. Therefore its origin is not in the harmony of the spheres, but rather in the music of the divine mind itself, and through its effect it can lead the listener directly to God Himself.[6]

---

[2] Quoted in Frances Yates, *The French Academies of the Sixteenth Century* (London: University of London, 1947; Nendeln: Kraus Reprint, 1968), 4.

[3] Ibid., 5.

[4] Ibid., 4.

[5] Ibid., 41.

[6] Ibid., 40.

Ficino's academy undoubtedly influenced many thinkers and artists in Florence and beyond. Other cities in Italy followed by organizing these evening adult discussion societies, and of course, a new one in the sixteenth century in Florence was an academy, known as the Camerata, which played so important a role in the birth of opera. During the sixteenth century another important one was organized in Paris, which we shall make reference to next. And in the eighteenth century, discussion groups, called salons, now organized by ladies in Paris played an important role in the French Revolution. Benjamin Franklin and Thomas Jefferson were both invited guests at these salons while living in Paris.

The most important commentary on aesthetics in music is found in the discussions of several academies formed in Paris in the second half of the sixteenth century. As with the academies in Italy, those in France were not educational institutions in the modern sense of the word, but more like high level gatherings of intellectuals for discussion and debate. A large part of their purpose was philological, attempting to raise French to a level of acceptance formerly enjoyed only by Latin.

It was in their relationship with the humanist movement that these academies played an influence on developments in the field of music. In France the Baïf Academy and the group known as the Pléiade were especially concerned with the liberal arts, and in particular the relationship of poetry and music. Because both the sixteenth century Italian and French intellectuals had taken from the ancient Greek writers a concept of music being closely related to the unseen organization of the world, it is no surprise that for them music included poetry and vice versa. Thus it was in the discussions of these academies that the Italians, under Bardi, moved toward monody and opera and the French, under Baïf, concentrated in making measured music fit measured poetry.

One of the foremost intellectual influences in Paris was the group of poets known as the Pléiade, led by Pierre de Ronsard.[7] This group seems to have come into formation at the College de Coqueret under Jean Dorat. Dorat was a charismatic lecturer on classical literature, who specialized in explaining how important truths were hidden in fables and poetry. The background of this view was the humanist belief that the ancient Greek artist was at once, musician, poet and a kind of prophet.

He attracted Ronsard and also Jean-Antoine de Baïf, son of Lazare de Baïf, an important literary advisor to François I, who would create the most famous of the academies. Dorat introduced his students to a wide variety of ancient and modern literature and apparently inspired considerable devotion. A contemporary observed that Ronsard would study until 2:00 AM and then awaken Baïf 'who rose and took the candle from him.'[8]

The informal meetings of these poets in the home of Baïf to discuss philosophy, rhetoric and poetry were a clear harbinger of the first important French academy, the *Académie de poésie et de musique*, formed by Baïf and Courville in 1570.

---

7   The members included Dorat, Ronsard, Du Bellay, Baïf, Belleau, Tyard, and Jodelle.

8   Quoted in Yates, Ibid., 14. One is reminded of the young Picasso who once shard a room with one bed with a burglar in Paris. Picasso worked during the day while the burglar slept and the burglar worked at night while Picasso slept.

The writings of the members of the Pléiade clearly testify to the humanistic aims of the group. Pontus de Tyard, wrote a treatise on music in which he testifies on behalf of the ethical impact of music.

> [Among the agents] music served as an exercise to temper the soul to a perfect condition of goodness and virtue, exciting and appeasing, by its native power and secret energy, the passions and affections, as the sounds were carried from the ear to the spiritual parts.[9]

Du Bellay, one of the most important poets of the group, wrote of their interest in sung poetry as the primary vehicle for their ethical goals.

> Sing to me those odes, yet unknown to the French muse, on a lute well tuned to the sound of the Greek and Roman lyre … Above all, take care that the type of poetry be far from the vulgar, enriched and made illustrious with proper words and vigorous epithets, adorned with grave sentences, and varied with all manner of colorful and poetic ornaments.[10]

The best known poet today, of those among the original Pléiade, was Pierre de Ronsard (1524–1585). We can see in him the strong humanist interest in ancient Greece.

> And, if I am able, I will reinstitute the use of the lyre, which in our day has been revived in Italy: which lyre alone should, and has the power to infuse soulful expression into verse and can give it the right weight of grave earnestness.[11]

Similarly, in his '*Abrégé de l'art poétique françois*' he speaks of the perceived Greek ideal of the combination of poetry and music.

> Poetry without instruments, or without the charm of a single or several voices, is just as little delightful as are instruments lacking the expressiveness of melody produced by a pleasant voice.[12]

And again, in one of his poems,

> To wed odes to the lyre,
> To know where the fingers stray on strings,
> Which song may well lie with them,
> And which tune may not be suited.[13]

---

[9] *Solitaire Second ou Discours de la Musique* (Lyons, 1552), quoted in Ibid., 41.

[10] Quoted in Gustave Reese, *Music in the Renaissance* (New York: Norton, 1959), 382.

[11] Quoted in François Lesure, *Musicians and Poets of the French Renaissance*, trans. Elio Gianturco (New York: Merlin Press, 1955), 56.

[12] Quoted in Ibid., 57.

[13] Quoted in Ibid., 55.

Another poem refers to an early deafness which hindered his own musicianship.

> I sing at times,
> But that is rare, for my voice is poor.[14]

Ronsard's most important statement on the view of aesthetics in music from the perspective of the Pléiade group is found in his dedication to François II of his *Livre des mélanges* (1560). Among other things we see here the new emphasis on the emotions, a subject so long feared by the Church.

> He that hearing a sweet accord of instruments or the sweetness of the natural voice feels no joy and no agitation and is not thrilled from head to foot, as being delightfully rapt and somehow carried out of himself—it is the sign of one whose soul is tortuous, vicious, and depraved, and of whom one should beware, as not fortunately born. For how could one be in accord with a man who by nature hates accord? He is unworthy to behold the sweet light of the sun who does not honor music as being a small part of that which, as Plato says, so harmoniously animates the whole great universe. On the contrary, he who does honor and reverence to music is commonly a man of worth, sound of soul, by nature loving things lofty, philosophy, the conduct of affairs of state, the tasks of war, and in brief, in all the honorable offices he ever shows the sparks of his virtue.[15]

Next he cites a number of the familiar myths and stories of music in ancient Greece and promises his royal patron that music will lighten his cares and allow him to return to his royal burden fresher and better disposed. Then Ronsard makes an interesting observation on the difference between the arts and science.

> The divine inspirations of music, poetry, and painting do not arrive at perfection by degrees, like the other sciences, but by starts, and like flashes of lightening, one here, another there, appear in various lands, then suddenly vanish. For that reason, when some excellent worker in this art reveals himself, you should guard him with care, as being something so excellent that it rarely appears.

He then lists a number of composers as examples of 'excellent workers in this art,' including des Prez, Willaert, Jannequin, Arcadelt, and Orlando Lassus, of whom he says 'seems alone to have stolen the harmony of the heavens to delight us with it on earth.'

The official beginning of Baïf's academy is acknowledged by the Letters Patent issued by Charles IX in 1570. The principal objective given in this document was to reestablish 'both the kind of poetry and the measure and rule of music anciently used by the Greeks and Romans.'[16] The document indicates that work and discussion along these lines had been in progress for three years, resulting in some progress in 'attempts at measured verses set to measured music.'

---

14 Quoted in Ibid., 54.
15 Quoted in Oliver Strunk, *Source Readings in Music History* (New York: Norton, 1950), 287.
16 Quoted in Yates, *The French Academies of the Sixteenth Century*, 21.

The academy was to consist of members in two categories: 'composers, singers and players' and listeners. The following statutes are very similar to, and unquestionably derived from, constitutions of the musician guilds of Paris and elsewhere. In particular, the musicians are to meet at specified times to rehearse together and separately, there is provision for sick members, a medallion is to be worn by the members (to be returned by his heirs upon his death) and finally, restrictions against quarrels and fighting amongst members—within one hundred feet of the meeting place.

Some of the language in this document is particularly interesting for its aesthetic insights. When performances are underway, in particular singing, the listeners must not speak, whisper, nor make any noise. No one can enter during a song, but must await its conclusion. It is interestingly that the listeners were not to approach the musicians in the private place where they prepared before the performances.

In a broader sense, Charles IX notes, in this same document, that his grandfather was a strong supporter of the arts and that in following suit he is acknowledging their importance to society. In particular, he states that in the opinion of the great legislators and philosophers among the ancients,

> it is of great importance for the morals of the citizens of a town that the music current and used in the country should be retained under certain laws, for the minds of most men are formed and their behavior influenced by its character, so that where music is disordered, there morals are also depraved, and where it is well ordered, there men are will disciplined morally.[17]

This is very similar to what we find in Baïf's own statutes for his academy, before he spells out his specific interest in recreating the supposed Greek union of text and music among the lyric poets.

> In order to bring back into use music in its perfection which is to represent words in singing completed by sounds, harmony and melody, consisting in the choice and regulation of voices, sounds and well harmonized accords, so as to produce the effect which the sense of the words requires, either lowering or raising or otherwise influencing the spirits, thus renewing the ancient fashion of composing measured verses to which are accommodated tunes likewise measured in accordance with the metric art.[18]

We find additional valuable information regarding the aesthetic purpose of Baïf's academy in the form of a document discovered by Yates, written early in the seventeenth century by the famous Marin Mersenne. It is apparently based on personal information given Mersenne by an older man who had been a member of the academy. This document is the principal source for our understanding that the academy studies ranged far beyond music and poetry.

---

[17] Quoted in Ibid., 23.

[18] Quoted in Ibid. It gives one pause that the impact of music on man is so little discussed today, as it was here and had been for two thousand years by the sixteenth century. Yates, the author of this brilliant book, in a comment which seems addressed more to our time, wryly adds here, 'Unless these phrases are meaningless verbiage, it would seem that … poetry and music was valued.'

> [The Academicians] did not wish to bring in a new kind of music, unless you call that new when something is restored to wholeness, but wished to recover those effects which, as we read, were once produced by the Greeks, by joining Gallic verses to our carefully cultivated music. For they hoped to exhilarate the depressed spirit, to reduce the over-elated spirit to modesty, and to stir themselves to other feelings by their own music …
>
> When Jean Antoine de Baïf and Joachim Thibault de Courville labored together to drive barbarism from Gaul, they considered that nothing would be of more potency for forming the manners of youth to everything honorable than if they were to recover the effects of ancient music and compose all their songs on the models of the fixed rules of the Greeks.
>
> Wherefore they wished so to provide that nothing should be lacking in the Academy which should make it suitable for the perfecting of a man, both in mind and body. Therefore they appointed to this Academy men most skilled in every kind of natural sciences, and instituted a prefect of it who should be called the Head Teacher. I leave out the other masters, of sciences, of tongues especially, of music, of poetry, of geography, of the various parts of mathematics, and of painting, who promoted the good of the mind, and the military prefects who taught all those things which are useful for military discipline and for the good of the body.[19]

The purpose of the academy to recreate the aesthetic aim of Greek music was to acquire the direct ethical effects of that music. As Yates observes,

> These artistic labors were undertaken, not for art's sake alone, but for certain effects which are expected of them. These melodies in the antique manner are believed to have the power of refining and purifying the minds of the listeners, and, through this purification, of initiating them into higher states of knowledge.[20]

So sure was Baïf that he had succeeded in this purpose, that six months after the official formation of his academy he wrote the king, Charles IX, requesting that he summon all the best musicians to a 'public competition' to demonstrate the superiority of the music of the new academy. He wanted to demonstrate that the purpose of this music was,

> not to leave the minds of the hearers where we find them, as most men of today maintain, but, according to the meaning of the words, to produce the three effects … namely to restrain, excite and calm the minds of the hearers who are deeply affected by the song, by means of the words, well-composed, well-sung, and carefully listened to.[21]

The goal of Baïf was clear, but a fatal problem remained. Since virtually no complete music exists from the period of the ancient Greek lyric poets, no one can know what this music was like, nor how they combined words and music.[22] In view of this fact, for all their study of the Greek texts, the Renaissance humanists could finally agree on only two conclusions: that the ethical impact must be centered in the words themselves and that the polyphonic Church style

---

[19] Quoted in Ibid., 24.

[20] Ibid., 36.

[21] Quoted in Ibid., 36.

[22] It is our belief the when the ancient philosophers speak of the correspondance of words and music they were actually speaking of the correspondance of the emotions of both, and not of a specific technique of melody, rhythm or harmony.

was therefore unacceptable, as one heard different words at the same time. This objection to polyphonic music was shared by nearly all humanists in Italy and France. A typical comment, here by Pontus de Tyard, one of the members of the Pléiade, reads,

> Music's purpose seems to be that of setting the word in such a fashion that anyone listening to it will become impassioned and carried away by the mood of the poet. The musician who knows how to deploy the solo voice to this end best attains his goal, in my opinion. Contrapuntal music most often brings to the ears only a lot of noise, from which you feel no vivid effect.[23]

Baïf is of interest as one of few people who went beyond simply pointing to the priority of words over music to actually proposing a specific method. His method, basically, was to attempt to coordinate the rhythm (long and short) of French verse [*vers mesures*] and the accompanying music [*musique mesurée*]. The text of the poetry therefore determined both the form and the rhythm of the music, resulting in a kind of chordal texture.[24] But while this can result in the emphasis of the words, it does not really have anything to do with enhancing the ethical or emotional impact of the experience. In fact, recent clinical evidence clearly demonstrates that it is melody, and not rhythm, which carries feeling content in music. Needless to say, Baif soon floundered in difficulties and one has to acknowledge that his theories, taken literally, had no future.[25] We might add, however, that Heartz points to a song by Courville, who was himself a singer, which was composed in the *musique mesurée* style, but was then highly ornamented, resulting not only in something more musical but in something equivalent to the monody tradition which developed from similar ideals in Italy.[26]

Regardless of the failure of the ideas of the academy to find much development in future music, a contemporary records that at least the academy was the source of fine concerts.

> It was in this pleasant residence that he had established an Academy where the best musicians in the world came in troops to accord the melodious sound of their instruments with that new cadence of measured verses which he had invented. The fame of these new and melodious concerts was so widespread that the King himself and all the princes of the court wished to hear them; and they did not disdain to divert themselves by often visiting our Baïf whom they found always in the company of the Muses or amongst the accords of music.[27]

---

[23] *Les Discours philosophiques* (Paris, 1587) quoted by Daniel Heartz, 'The Chanson in the Humanist Era,' in *Current thought in Musicology* (Austin: University of Texas Press, 1976), 227.

[24] Reese, *Music in the Renaissance*, 383, identifies the *Le Printemps* of Claude Le Jeune (1525–1600), composed to the poetry of Baïf, as an example of music composed according to these principles. After the academies were closed, Eustache Du Caurroy (1549–1609) was still composing according to the ideals of musique mesurée.

[25] Yates, *The French Academies of the Sixteenth Century*, 52ff, discusses the inherent difficulties faced by Baïf.

[26] Heartz, 'The Chanson in the Humanist Era,' 215.

[27] Scevole de Sainte Marthe, quoted in Yates, *The French Academies of the Sixteenth Century*, 20.

Another contemporary, d'Aubigne, reports of hearing at the academy a performance which included 'an excellent concert of guitars, twelve viols, four spinets, four lutes, two pandoras and two theorboes.'[28]

One composer influenced by Baïf was Claude Le Jeune, who in the preface to his 'Printemps,' deplored that the ancient art of the Greeks had been lost and that his purpose was to restore music to its rightful place that it might stir 'the soul of man to such passions as [the Greeks] intended.'[29] One of his contemporaries, Odet de la Noue, believed he had been successful, for he writes in a eulogy,

> by the efforts of his melody he flings out soul wherever he pleases;
> He casts it down to grievous death, or stirs it up to joy;
> He instills courage into the most dejected heart;
> And to raving men he restores meekness.[30]

To these lofty ideals there were, as there always are, detractors. Some worried that there might be composed songs against the honor of the king or of France. The faculty of the University of Paris was of course jealous and concerned that their role was being usurped. Growing efforts to eliminate the academy were eventually silenced by the king himself and interestingly enough this ultimatum was addressed to the Faculty of Medicine.[31]

Under Henry III a similar academy, known as the Palace Academy, came into being and it is not clear if it was entirely separate from Baïf's group or consisted of the same people.[32] Both academies, however, came to an end about 1584, due to the civil wars resulting from the religious turmoil.

It is somewhat of a surprise to find Henry III, whose character is so criticized by some contemporaries, described by one early writer as,

> always in the company of the Muses and amongst the sweet accords of the children of music, for he loved music and had a marvelous understanding of it. This liberal and magnificent prince gave a handsome remuneration and accorded him from time to time newly created offices and certain confiscations which procured for Baif the means of maintaining in their studies several men of letters, of entertaining in his house all the learned men of the age, and of dispensing much hospitality.[33]

---

28 Quoted in Reese, *Music in the Renaissance*, 566.

29 Quoted in Lesure, *Musicians and Poets of the French Renaissance*, 111.

30 Quoted in Ibid., 112.

31 The reader is reminded that Apollo was the god of both music and medicine.

32 The Palace Academy was apparently organized by 1576 and among whose attending were three members of the original Pleiade poets, Ronsard, Tyard and Baif.

33 Guillaume Colletet, quoted in Yates, *The French Academies of the Sixteenth Century*, 29.

In any case, the Palace Academy seems to have been more centered in philosophy than music. An Englishman who visited on one occasion, described the members as discussing, for as much as four hours at a time, '*de primis causis de sensu et sensibiliti.*'[34] Needless to say, with the affairs of state in growing disarray, Henry III came under considerable criticism for spending his time in such discussion.

In the following century, under Louis XIV, several academies where established under the auspices of the state. One of these, the Academy of Music, was given by the king to Lully to administer and he turned it into a means of controlling large-scale productions in Paris.

---

34   Quoted in Ibid., 33.

Bibliography

CHAPTER 1 MACHAUT ON MUSIC

Figg, Kristen. *The Short Lyric Poems of Jean Froissart*. New York: Garland Publishing, 1994.

Jacques de Liege. *Speculum Musicae*. In F. Joseph Smith, 'Ars Nova—A Re-Definition?' *Musica Disciplina*, XVIII (1964).

Le Livre du Voir-Dit de Guillaume de Machaut. Paris: Paulin Paris, 1875.

Machaut, Guillaume de. *Oeuvres*. Edited by Ernest Hoepffner. Paris, 1908–21.

Machaut, Guillaume de. *Musikalische Werke*. Edited by Friedrich Ludwig. Leipzig, 1926.

Machaut, Guillaume de. *Remede de Fortune*. Translated by James Wimsatt and William Kibler. Athens: The University of Georgia Press, 1988.

Machaut, Guillaume de. *The Tale of the Alerion*. Translated by Minnette Gaudet and Constance Hieatt. Toronto: University of Toronto Press, 1994.

Machaut, Guillaume de. *The Judgment of the King of Navarre*. Barton Palmer. New York: Garland Publishing, 1988.

Machaut, Guillaume de. *Le Jugement du roy de Behaigne*. James Wimsatt and William Kibler. Athens: The University of Georgia Press, 1988.

Machaut, Guillaume de. *La Prise d'Alexandre*. Edited by L. de Mas Latrie. Geneva, 1877.

Page, Christopher. 'Machaut's 'Pupil' Deschamps on the Performance of Music.' *Early Music* 5, no. 4 (1977): 484–491, doi: 10.1093/earlyj/5.4.484

Pisan, Christine. *Le Livre des Fais et Bonnes Meurs du Sage Roy Charles V*. Edited by S. Solente. Paris, 1936.

CHAPTER 2 PETRARCH ON MUSIC

D'Amico, John. *Renaissance Humanism in Papal Rome*. Baltimore: Johns Hopkins University Press.

Larner, John. *Culture and Society in Italy, 1290–1420*. New York: Scribner's, 1971.

Petrarch. *Petrarch's Bucolicum Carmen*. Translated by Thomas Bergin. New Haven: Yale University Press, 1974.

Petrarch *Letters from Petrarch*. Translated by Morris Bishop. Bloomington: Indiana University Press, 1966.

Petrarch. *Petrarch's Lyric Poems*. Transl;ated by Robert Durling. Cambridge: Harvard University Press, 1976.

Petrarch. *Remedies for Fortune Fair and Foul*. Translated by Conrad Rawski. Bloomington: Indiana University Press, 1991.

Robinson, James. *Petrarch, The First modern Scholar and Man of Letters*. New York: Putnam, 1914.

Chapter 3 Giovanni Boccaccio on Music

Boccaccio, Giovanni. *Genealogia Deorum Gentilium.* Quoted in *Boccaccio on Poetry.* Translated by Charles Osgood. New York: The Liberal Arts Press, 1956.

Boccaccio, Giovanni. *The Decameron.* Translated by Mark Musa and Peter Bondanella. New York: Norton, 1977.

Boccaccio, Giovanni. *The Fates of Illustrious Men.* Translated by Louis Hall. New York: Ungar, 1965.

Boccaccio, Giovanni. *Concerning Famous Women.* Translated by Guido Guarino. New Brunswick: Rutgers University Press, 1963.

Boccaccio, Giovanni. *The Corbaccio.* Translated by Anthony Cassell. Urbana: University of Illinois Press, 1975.

Boccaccio, Giovanni. *Theseus.* Translated by Bernadette McCoy. New York: Medieval Text Association, 1974.

Boccaccio, Giovanni. *Filostrato.* Translated by Nathaniel Griffin and Arthur Myrick New York: Bilbo and Tannen, 1967.

Boccaccio, Giovanni. *Amorous Fiammetta.* Translated by Edward Hutton. Westport: Greenwood Press, 1926.

Chapter 4 Geoffrey Chaucer on Music

Chaucer, Geoffrey. *The Complete Works of Geoffrey Chaucer.* Boston: Houghton Mifflin, 1933.

Goldron, Romain. *Minstrels and Masters.* H. S. Stuttman.

Salmen, Walter. *Der Fahrende Musiker im Europaischen Mittelalter.* Kassel, 1960.

Chapter 5 Leonardo da Vinci on Music

Blunt, Anthony. *Artistic Theory in Italy, 1450–1600.* Oxford: Clarendon Press, 1959.

da Vinci, Leonardo. *The Literary Works of Leonardo da Vinci.* Edited by jean Paul Richter. London: Phaidon, 1970.

Giovio, Paolo. *Leonardi Vencii Vita* [1528].

Lomazzo. *Idea del Tempio della Pittura* [1590].

Chapter 6 Baldassare Castiglione on Music

Castiglione, Baldassare. *The Courtier.* Translated by George Bull. New York: Penguin Books.

Chapter 7 Michelangelo on Art and Music

Armenini, Giovan Battista. *De' veri precetti della pittura.* Ravenna, 1586.

Blunt, Anthony. *Artistic Theory in Italy, 1450–1600.* Oxford: Clarendon Press, 1959.

Chantelou, M. *Journal du voyage du Cavalier Bernini.* Paris, 1885.

Clements, Robert J. *Michelangelo; A Self-Portrait*. New York: New York University Press, 1968.
Doni, Anton Francesco. *Disegno*. Venice, 1549.
Michelangelo. *Complete Poems of Michelangelo*. Translated by Creighton Gilbert. Princeton: Princeton University Press, 1963.
Michelangelo. *The Letters of Michelangelo*. Translated by E. H. Ramsden. Stanford: Stanford University Press, 1963.

CHAPTER 8 GIROLAMO CARDANO ON MUSIC

Hieronymi Cardani Mediolensis.
Miller, Clement. *Hieronymus Cardanus, Writings on Music*. [Rome]: American Institute of Musicology, 1973.
Ore, Oystein. *Cardano The Gambling Scholar*. New York: Dover, 1953.
Wykes, Alan. *Doctor Cardano*. London, 1969.

CHAPTER 9 ERASMUS ON MUSIC

Allen, P. S. *Erasmus*. Oxford, 1934.
Erasmus. *The Collected Works of Erasmus*. Toronto: University of Toronto Press, 1992.
Erasmus. *The Colloquies of Erasmus*. Translated by Craig Thompson. Chicago: University of Chicago Press, 1965.
Glarean, Heinrich. *The Dodecachordon of Heinrich Glarean*. Edited by Clement Miller. American Institute of Musicology, 1965.
Hallett, P. E. *The Life and Illustrious Martyrdom of Sir Thomas More*. London, 1928.
Miller, Clement A. 'Erasmus on Music.' *The Musical Quarterly* 52, no. 3 (July, 1966): 332–349, http://www.jstor.org/stable/3085961

CHAPTER 10 THE ACADEMIES

Corsi, Giovanni. *The Life of Marsilio Ficino*. Faculty, Language Department, School of Economic Science, London.
Heartz, Daniel. 'The Chanson in the Humanist Era.' In *Current thought in Musicology*. Austin: University of Texas Press, 1976.
Lesure, François. *Musicians and Poets of the French Renaissance*. New York: Merlin Press, 1955.
Reese, Gustave. *Music in the Renaissance*. New York: Norton, 1959. Strunk, Oliver. *Source Readings in Music History*. New York: Norton, 1950.
Yates, Frances. *The French Academies of the Sixteenth Century*. London: University of London, 1947; Nendeln: Kraus Reprint, 1968.

About the Author

Dr. David Whitwell is a graduate ('with distinction') of the University of Michigan and the Catholic University of America, Washington DC (PhD, Musicology, Distinguished Alumni Award, 2000) and has studied conducting with Eugene Ormandy and at the Akademie für Musik, Vienna. Prior to coming to Northridge, Dr. Whitwell participated in concerts throughout the United States and Asia as Associate First Horn in the USAF Band and Orchestra in Washington DC, and in recitals throughout South America in cooperation with the United States State Department.

At the California State University, Northridge, which is in Los Angeles, Dr. Whitwell developed the CSUN Wind Ensemble into an ensemble of international reputation, with international tours to Europe in 1981 and 1989 and to Japan in 1984. The CSUN Wind Ensemble has made professional studio recordings for BBC (London), the Köln Westdeutscher Rundfunk (Germany), NOS National Radio (The Netherlands), Zürich Radio (Switzerland), the Television Broadcasting System (Japan) as well as for the United States State Department for broadcast on its 'Voice of America' program. The CSUN Wind Ensemble's recording with the Mirecourt Trio in 1982 was named the 'Record of the Year' by The Village Voice. Composers who have guest conducted Whitwell's ensembles include Aaron Copland, Ernest Krenek, Alan Hovhaness, Morton Gould, Karel Husa, Frank Erickson and Vaclav Nelhybel.

Dr. Whitwell has been a guest professor in 100 different universities and conservatories throughout the United States and in 23 foreign countries (most recently in China, in an elite school housed in the Forbidden City). Guest conducting experiences have included the Philadelphia Orchestra, Seattle Symphony Orchestra, the Czech Radio Orchestras of Brno and Bratislava, The National Youth Orchestra of Israel, as well as resident wind ensembles in Russia, Israel, Austria, Switzerland, Germany, England, Wales, The Netherlands, Portugal, Peru, Korea, Japan, Taiwan, Canada and the United States.

He is a past president of the College Band Directors National Association, a member of the Prasidium of the International Society for the Promotion of Band Music, and was a member of the founding board of directors of the World Association for Symphonic Bands and Ensembles (WASBE). In 1964 he was made an honorary life member of Kappa Kappa Psi, a national professional music fraternity. In September, 2001, he was a delegate to the UNESCO Conference on Global Music in Tokyo. He has been knighted by sovereign organizations in France, Portugal and Scotland and has been awarded the gold medal of Kerkrade, The Netherlands, and the silver medal of Wangen, Germany, the highest honor given wind conductors in the United States, the medal of the Academy of Wind and Percussion Arts (National Band Association) and the highest honor given wind conductors in Austria, the gold medal of the Austrian Band Association. He is a member of the Hall of Fame of the California Music Educators Association.

Dr. Whitwell's publications include more than 127 articles on wind literature including publications in Music and Letters (London), the London Musical Times, the Mozart-Jahrbuch (Salzburg), and 52 books, among which is his 13-volume *History and Literature of the Wind Band and Wind Ensemble* and an 8-volume series on *Aesthetics in Music*. In addition to numerous modern editions of early wind band music his original compositions include 5 symphonies.

David Whitwell was named as one of six men who have determined the course of American bands during the second half of the 20th century, in the definitive history, *The Twentieth Century American Wind Band* (Meredith Music).

A doctoral dissertation by German Gonzales (2007, Arizona State University) is dedicated to the life and conducting career of David Whitwell through the year 1977. David Whitwell is one of nine men described by Paula A. Crider in *The Conductor's Legacy* (Chicago: GIA, 2010) as 'the legendary conductors' of the 20th century.

> 'I can't imagine the 2nd half of the 20th century—without David Whitwell and what he has given to all of the rest of us.' Frederick Fennell (1993)

About the Editor

CRAIG DABELSTEIN began studying the piano at age seven and took up the saxophone at age twelve. Mr Dabelstein has Bachelor of Arts (Music) and Bachelor of Music degrees from the Queensland Conservatorium of Music, where he majored in the performance of classical saxophone repertoire. He also has a Graduate Diploma of Learning and Teaching and a Graduate Certificate in Editing and Publishing from the University of Southern Queensland.

He has held the principal alto and tenor saxophone chairs in the Australian Wind Orchestra and has been an augmenting member of the Queensland Philharmonic Orchestra, the Queensland Symphony Orchestra, and the Queensland Pops Orchestra. For many years he was also a member of the Queensland Saxophone Quartet.

He has been a casual conductor of the Young Conservatorium Symphonic Winds, and has previously been a saxophone teacher at the Queensland Conservatorium of Music. He is a regular conductor of the Queensland Wind Orchestra, having served as their artistic director and chief conductor from 2004 to 2009.

Craig Dabelstein is a research associate for the *Teaching Music Through Performance in Band* series of books, contributing analyses to volumes 7, 8, 1 (rev. edn), and the *Solos with Wind Band Accompaniment* volume. He served as the copyeditor and layout designer of the *Australian Clarinet and Saxophone Magazine* from 2007 to 2009 and he has written many CD and book reviews for *Music Forum* magazine. He is the editor of the second editions of the books by Dr. David Whitwell including *A Concise History of the Wind Band*, *Foundations of Music Education*, *Music Education of the Future*, *The Sousa Oral History Project*, *Wagner on Bands*, *Berlioz on Bands*, *The Art of Musical Conducting*, and the *Aesthetics of Music* series (8 volumes) and *The History and Literature of the Wind Band and Wind Ensemble* series (13 volumes). From 1994 to 2012 he was a staff member at Brisbane Girls Grammar School. He now teaches woodwinds and conducts bands at St. Joseph's College, Gregory Terrace, Brisbane, Australia.